Tonka

Dennis David
and Lloyd Laumann

MBI

First published in 2004 by MBI, an imprint of MBI Publishing Company, Galtier Plaza, Suite 200, 380 Jackson Street, St. Paul, MN 55101-3885 USA

MBI titles are also available at discounts in bulk quantity for industrial or sales-promotional use. For details write to Special Sales Manager at Motorbooks International Wholesalers & Distributors, Galtier Plaza, Suite 200, 380 Jackson Street, St. Paul, MN 55101-3885 USA.

ISBN 0-7603-1868-9

Printed in China

Acquisitions Editor: Dennis Pernu

On cover: Mighty Dump and Loader.

On the frontispiece: 1973 No. 3885 Mighty Tonka Winnebago. *Lee Klancher*

On the title page: Feature Road Grader. *Lee Klancher*

On the back cover 1: The No. 0950-6 Suburban Pumper was a great toy to play with (or annoy your brother) on a hot summer day in 1956. *Lloyd L. Laumann collection*

On the back cover 2: 1969 No. 2900 Mighty Dump. *Lee Klancher*

On the back cover 3: 1949 No. 20 Power Lift Truck. *Lee Klancher*

CONTENTS

Acknowledgments

The creation of a book is never without an intense effort that occupies vast amounts of time. That time usually comes at the expense of something else. In this case, I need to thank my wife Susan for giving me the time and encouragement to complete this project. I also need to give my son Christopher credit for giving me uninterrupted peace for hours on end.

I would like to thank the following people for their help with some of the photos and information that helped make this book possible. Special thanks to Lloyd Laumann and the many former employees of the Mound, Minnesota, Tonka Toy plant for all of their time and knowledge. Thanks to Lee Klancher for taking photos of Lloyd's collection. Thanks also to Mike George from Autoworks Unlimited, and Brian Kane for allowing me to photograph some of the pieces in their collections. Thanks to Ted Tietz Jr. for the on-location shots. The folks at MBI were also great to work with, and credit goes to Dennis Pernu for the initial idea on the history of the Tonka Toy Company. Amy Glaser edited this book and did a great job. Julie Duffy from Hasbro Inc., supplied some present day information, and I thank her as well.

A special thanks also goes to all of my family. Mom and Dad, brother Doug, and sister Sharon have always known me as "that kid who likes to take everything apart," and I thank them for their never-ending support.

—Dennis David

1955 Carnation Milk Truck.
Dennis David

6

Twenty years of interviewing former Tonka employees and their relatives; searching for Tonka toys, catalogs, advertisements, and information have culminated in this book. Dennis David, as well as Dennis Pernu and Amy Glaser of MBI Publishing Company, have been the motivating and guiding forces in this book.

Thanks to hundreds of former Tonka employees who provided information and allowed me to purchase toys, literature, and memorabilia. Special thanks goes to the former Tonka employees who participated in interviews with Dennis David.

I would not have been involved in collecting toys or writing about Tonka's history without the initial motivation and inspiration of Ron Cadieux. Sue Cathers was instrumental in providing the contact with Dennis David.

Three people have been an integral part of my hobby and deserve special attention. My wife Jean, daughter Ann, and son Gregg. During the early years of my hobby, they graciously attended toy shows with me and willingly traveled out of state to attend shows and trudged through antique shops. Jean was most involved in the written information I have published in the past 20 years, some of which is included in this book, by editing all of my written material. Her patience, understanding, and input have been truly extraordinary.

Space and the fear of unintentionally omitting the name of a former employee or hobbyist prevents me from listing all the people who have been instrumental in the publication of this book. Most importantly, thanks to God for the opportunity to be associated with so many caring, supportive human beings!

I would like to dedicate this book to all the former hardworking, conscientious employees who made Tonka one of the best toy companies in the world.

–Lloyd Laumann

1970 Tiny Pickup.
Lee Klancher

Preface

At 9:30 p.m. on October 27, 1982, Lloyd Laumann, Tonka's vice president of manufacturing, slipped behind the wheel of his 1978 Pontiac and started the car. It was a Wednesday evening, and the Minnesota skies were overcast. The summer leaves had turned, and the harsh winter would soon be upon the region. Lloyd had just exited Tonka's main assembly plant where he was responsible for all of the manufacturing departments, as well as several other support areas. Turning onto Shoreline Drive, he glanced at the shores of Lake Minnetonka and continued west on County Road 110. On most days he listened to the radio and took his time driving home, but tonight was different. He was in a hurry. On most working days he would have been home hours ago, but his business on this day had kept him at the plant well into the evening hours. The drive from the plant to his home was a mere 11 miles, but tonight the drive seemed like an eternity.

He turned south onto County Road 92 and hardly noticed that his foot was pushing heavily onto the accelerator. He had taken this route home a thousand times before and he knew the roads well, but he was now painfully aware that he would not be traveling this route for much longer. Speeding down a stretch of County Road 92 through the village of Saint Bonifacius, he was traveling at 55 miles per hour in an area with a posted speed limit of 30. Looking back on it, he said, "I shouldn't have even been driving that day, and I certainly shouldn't have been driving that fast."

A patrol officer of the Minnetrista Police Department was working his usual shift that night. From his vantage point from the side of County Road 92, he could spot speeders coming down the hill into Saint Bonifacius. When he saw Lloyd's Pontiac, it was obvious to him that the driver was not paying attention to the speed limit. As the car flew by him, the officer started his patrol car, switched on his lights, and gave pursuit. Lloyd estimates that he drove for about a half-mile before he noticed the flashing lights of the patrol car, but when he did, he immediately pulled over to the side and stepped out of his car. The officer also stepped out of his patrol car and expected the usual "in a

1956 Suburban Pumper No. 0950-6
Lee Klancher

hurry" excuse or maybe even an intoxicated driver, but what he encountered was a man emotionally drained. In a kind gesture of concern, the officer invited Lloyd to the patrol car where they talked for a few minutes. It didn't take long for the officer to understand the problem, and he also shared Lloyd's concern. The news was not good, and soon everyone would know.

Lloyd had spent the past five hours communicating some very bad news to many of his friends and coworkers. It was his task to tell them that Tonka's entire production operation was being moved to Texas and Mexico and that the Mound, Minnesota, facility would close at the end of 1983. Lloyd's intentions were simple; he wanted to get home after 14 hours at the plant before the 10:00 p.m. news and eat dinner. After hearing Lloyd's story, the officer allowed him to go with simple instructions to obey the speed limit and drive safely. Lloyd continued on in silence and realized that this police officer may have just saved his life, but there was nothing anyone could do about the thousands of jobs that would leave with Tonka Toys.

When my editor Dennis Pernu and I first talked about a book on the Tonka Toy Company, the first step was to see if there was actually a story out there and then see if there was enough information to put the story together. I made many calls and talked with many people, including Sue Cathers from the Westonka Historical Society. She gave me the phone number of a person who might know a little about the company, and that phone number belonged to Lloyd Laumann. That phone number led to this book.

Lloyd and I spoke several times over the phone, and it quickly became apparent that Lloyd had a vision of a book on Tonka's history that was very similar to my own. The book we wanted to create would not be a collector's price guide nor a simple explanation of Tonka's history. Instead it would engage all facets of the Tonka story and place a key emphasis on the people that made it possible. With several phone calls behind us, there was only one thing left to do. I booked a flight from my home on the East Coast and headed to Minnesota to meet Lloyd and discuss the possibility of the project.

I will never forget our first meeting. Lloyd had been approached about a book on the Tonka Toy Company several times, but none had come to fruition. As a former Tonka employee of almost 30 years, he had the experience and paperwork, and he recalled Tonka's glory days in the Mound, Minnesota, region. I knew I had found the right person when Lloyd took me into his office, which was a small room in the downstairs floor of his home. In the corner of a room covered with Tonka products and artifacts was the very desk that Russell Wenkstern, known by many as "Mr. Tonka," had used in his early years at Tonka. The Tonka identification asset plate was still firmly attached to the desk.

Over the course of the next few days, Lloyd, my son Chris, and I met many times. We had lunch, talked over ideas, and even rode out to the former Tonka Plant in Mound, which still exists but is occupied by other industrial concerns. As we walked, Lloyd explained with great enthusiasm how the toys were built. He pointed out where raw steel was delivered, where press machines punched out parts, and where finished toys were stored and readied for shipment. It quickly became apparent that Lloyd had a passion for his years at Tonka and the story needed to be told. Lloyd's collection of paperwork from the Minnesota years is vast and comprehensive. Some of his papers are the only known copies to exist. I came home with a renewed sense of enthusiasm for the project, and I immediately called my editor and said, "I think we've got a great story here."

This brings us to where we are today. Not only did I meet the person who I would collaborate with on this book, but I also met a new friend. A man who shares the same vision as I do of what the Tonka story is all about. In the end, it's not about the success of Tonka or about how many Tonka trucks were ever built. It's about American workers and the stories they have to tell. This book is dedicated to those many employees of Tonka's Mound, Minnesota, plant, and it is my sincere hope that this book does justice to the story they have to tell.

—Dennis David

Chapter 1

1946–1947

FROM THE VERY START OF CHILDHOOD, TOYS SERVE TO ENHANCE THE IMAGINATION, CREATE DREAMS, and build whole new worlds. Toy manufacturing as we know it in the modern world can be traced back to the industrial revolution, for here lies the heart and soul of the manufacturing techniques that gave rise to mass production. As production rose, prices dropped, and average children could now own a toy of their own. A toy boat was no longer exclusively the product of an exotic manufacturer like Gubruder Marlin of Germany, or a toy train the work of Hornby Dublo of England.

Fastforward to the years immediately after World War II. America's mighty industrial machine had just finished the largest retooling and manufacturing endeavor in the history of the world. With the war over, all of these companies now had to retool once again for a peacetime economy. World War II had changed the face of America's machines, and factories that had built guns and bombers now had to scramble to come up with new products that appealed to customers. For America's car builders, returning to automobile production required nothing more than an updated design. But companies such as Lionel and Max, who built products for the war effort, now had to find new products that would ensure their survival.

1945 Streater Steam Shovel.
Lloyd L. Laumann collection

Tonka logo from 1947-1955.
Lloyd L. Laumann collection

After World War II, there was a demand for consumer goods the likes of which America had never seen. Cars, tires, stoves, refrigerators, radios, and furniture were items that America had been living without for a number of years. It was a time of unheard-of spending and unprecedented demand. People needed things, and the great American machine stood ready to deliver. With the GIs returning home with several months of back pay, America was about to enter its golden years. The return of thousands of American servicemen immediately rekindled old relationships that resulted in a flurry of marriages. Although it may not have been apparent in the immediate postwar years, those renewed relationships created a new generation of Americans, and the baby boomers needed toys.

This is where our story begins. Not in the industrial confines of the Ford Motor Company, and not in the famous toy stores of New York or Chicago, but in Mound, Minnesota, a small town on the shores of Lake Minnetonka. It was there that a few people gathered and began a small company with an eye on manufacturing products that consumers would buy and a hope of turning a profit along the way. What started as a small manufacturer eventually grew into the largest producer of toy trucks that the world would ever know.

The word "Tonka" comes from the Dakota-Sioux word meaning "great." Mound, Minnesota, was a small community of about 2,000 people in 1946 and became the work-force foundation for the Tonka Toy company.

The Tonka story begins with three men and a vision. The original intent of these three may not have been to become the nation's largest toy manufacturer, but as events unfolded, they catered to the demands of consumers. Avery F. Crounse, Lynn E. Baker, and Alvin F. Tesch were the founding fathers of the Tonka Toy Company. The earliest Tonka logo carries

Lynn E. Baker 1899-1964
Lloyd L. Laumann collection

Avery F. Crounse, 1880-1960
Lloyd L. Laumann collection

Alvin F. Tesch, 1915-2000
Lloyd L. Laumann collection

the theme of three gulls, each signifying the vision of these men. A chance meeting between these three created the foundation for one of the greatest toy companies in the world, but before we get too far ahead, let's go back to the very beginning.

Avery F. Crounse was an educated man. He graduated from the University of Minnesota in 1903, and his guidance and knowledge created the very cornerstone of the new company. He was not a young man in the formative years of Tonka, but his wisdom was a guiding force in placing the company on firm ground. His degree in mechanical engineering enabled him to work in the construction industry for many years, but the depression caused him to seek work in other venues. At one time, he operated mining properties in Mexico and Montana.

In the 1920s, Crounse had a chance encounter that would forever change his life, as well as the lives of million of others. Crounse purchased a grand Auburn sport sedan from a used-car dealership. The car salesman's name was Lynn E. Baker, and the sale solidified a friendship between these two men that would last a lifetime. They became such good friends that Crounse provided Baker with financial support for the purchase of a car dealership. Baker operated the Tri-Motor Company, a Studebaker dealership on Lake Street in Minneapolis, for several years. The two men continued their business relationship through the 1930s, and after World War II they began to formulate the plan for a company special-

Old schoolhouse building that was the first building for Mound Metalcraft.
Lloyd L. Laumann collection

izing in stamping metal. Crounse had the business savvy, and Baker was an excellent salesman. The only component missing was a good tool-and-die man. That missing component soon turned up in one of Crounse's business ventures.

In the early 1940s, Crounse became involved with the Industrial Tool and Die Company in Minneapolis. It was here that he discovered the talents of a young man named Alvin F. Tesch. Tesch was somewhat of a manufacturing genius and always figured out ways to do things faster and better. Crounse was so impressed with Tesch that the two became friends, and Tesch would become the third gull on the Tonka label. Baker had moved from selling cars to selling machines for Industrial Tool and Die Company, and the three men now possessed the marketing, tooling, and business skills that led to the Tonka Toy Company.

The postwar boom of consumer products in the late 1940s gave rise to hundreds of new small businesses. Demand for new products was at an unheard of level, and the time was ripe for the introduction of a new company. Crounse and Baker began discussing the formation of a metal stamping company to serve the needs of several businesses in the area. All they needed was a facility, and Crounse found an old school building in Mound, which became the first home of Tonka Toys.

LeRoy Schafer

LeRoy Schafer never actually applied for a job at Tonka. He landed his job by knowing the right people. "Russ Wenkstern was my neighbor, and he asked me if I would drive a Chevy stake-body truck for Tonka," he said. Thus began a career that lasted for 39 years. Schafer performed many different jobs at Tonka. "That's what I liked about it—there were always so many different things to do."

Schafer drove the Chevy truck for Tonka for several years, and he then drove a forklift and moved parts and materials around. He also worked in inventory control and finally ended up as a receiving supervisor for Tonka. "In the early years at the schoolhouse, receiving would get little more than a few deliveries a day, but by the late 1960s, receiving was a very busy place," he said.

When production moved from Mound, Schafer was one of the lucky ones Tonka retained to work at the corporate office. The headquarters still had a small pickup truck that Schafer used to run errands. It all came full circle given the fact that Russ Wenkstern himself hired Schafer to drive a truck, which turned out to be his last job there. Schafer is among the many Tonka employees that speak very highly of the work force from those years. "We had a lot of fun, but we always got the work done."

The school was built in 1908 and was quite large for its time. With three floors, tall ceilings, and sturdy brick walls, it was a solid structure. Sadly, it was torn down in 1971 to make way for a new post office and a small shopping center. The Mound Metalcraft Company was not the first manufacturing concern to call the school home. At the time of Crounse's interest in the school building, it was home to the Streater Company, a manufacturer of several different products. Most notably, Streater built ammunition boxes during World War II, and then manufactured retail store fixtures. Streater also built wooden toys. Although their wooden toys weren't as durable as the classic pressed-steel Tonka Toys that would appear a few years later, they still gave children a way to fulfill their imagination.

Upon Crounse's inspection of the school building Streater offered for sale, he noted the structural integrity of the building was good. Its basement offered the space needed for the large, heavy metal-stamping machines. The basement also provided the ideal location for future paint lines and drying ovens. The school building offered a large freight elevator that was perfect for moving large objects, vast quantities of components, and finished products from one floor to another. The deal was solidified, and the old schoolhouse became the new home of Mound Metalcraft. The sale price of the building was the grand sum of $7,500.

In a letter to his sister dated August 31, 1946, Crounse explains the complexities involved in the start-up of the new company.

"The Mound deal is progressing, but slowly and satisfactorily. It's hard to go faster with all of us so busy, but we are getting a lot of the preliminary steps taken care of. It is going to be difficult to line up the machinery and materials we will need, and we are working on that now. Also, we are having our dies made, or rather we are making them ourselves."

At the time the letter was written, Baker was gathering machinery, Tesch was busy preparing designs for several new products, and Crounse was working around the clock staying on top of the details. On September 18, 1946, Mound Metalcraft Incorporated was created with the three men as partners. Records indicate that each man invested $5,000 in the new venture, and Crounse invested another $40,000 to begin production.

The three men now had to assign titles and positions to themselves. Always the excellent salesman, Lynn Baker was appointed the president of the new company. Alvin Tesch, with his vast experience in toolmaking and manufacturing, was selected by Crounse to become the vice president and works manager. Crounse was named secretary and treasurer.

Mound Metalcraft's first products consisted of two different styles of tie racks, identified as clipper-tie valets. Originally, Baker planned for a major output of hoes; rakes; shovels; and tie, shoe, and hat racks, in addition to the contracted stamping business to serve as the primary base for the company's revenue. The tie racks were a rather simple affair consisting of a flat steel plate with 12 spring clips. The only difference between the two models was the finish on the steel plate. One had a smooth chrome finish, and the other had a machine-burled finish. The tie rack was mounted by two wood screws that went through two holes in the rack and into the wall. The racks were made from a sturdy piece of metal and would outlast any tie they held. Examples turn up at estate sales every now and then, although most who see them are unaware of their historic significance. Contrary to popular belief, the garden tools and closet accessories were never manufactured in marketable quantities, and it is doubtful that one would turn up anywhere.

Clipper-tie valet.
Lee Klancher

Profile
Muriel Reinitz

Many of the women employed at Tonka worked what were called "nontraditional" jobs. One of those employees was Muriel Reinitz, who, during a portion of her 30 years at Tonka, was responsible for ensuring that the plastic parts for Tonka's toys were of the highest standards. As an employee of the Tool Room, she and five other women were mold polishers. When a part was molded through plastic injection, there were sometimes remnants left over that clogged the holes or failed to release from the mold. Muriel and her counterparts would clean and polish the molds so they could be reused. If the molds were not properly cleaned and polished, there would be a hole or a line where there wasn't supposed to be one. "We did a lot of windshields and clear plastic parts, so they had to be perfect," Reinitz said. Her department was part of Tool & Die Room, which was predominantly occupied by men. She says it was a little unusual for women to be in that department during that era, but "We all got along well together, and I know that our efforts made a big difference in the quality of our toys at Tonka," she said.

Muriel and several of her Tonka friends still get together to reminisce. "I certainly learned a lot about polishing, but I also learned how to spot weld." Of all of Muriel's years at Tonka, her fondest memories are of the Christmas parties, where all of the employees brought their children into the plant. As one of Tonka's early employees, Muriel remembers working at the old schoolhouse during the hot summers. Occasionally, on hot summer afternoons, the employees would sit on the hillside by the school and eat fresh-cut watermelon that was supplied by Tonka. "There were a lot of dedicated people at Tonka, and it really was like one big happy family."

1947 No. 150 Crane & Clam.
Lloyd L Laumann collection

In 1946, Streater introduced a line of metal toys at the New York Toy Fair. A Steam Shovel and a Crane & Clam shell digger were unveiled, but both received minimal enthusiasm from prospective buyers. Streater lacked an enthusiastic salesperson to push the product. Company president Ed Streater was disappointed with consumer reaction and returned to Spring Park, where he kept the company's focus on its line of store fixtures. The dies for the new toy line went into storage. In the meantime, Crounse, Baker, and Tesch heard about Streater's new metal toy line and decided it might be the product they needed as a diversified sideline to back up planned garden-tool and closet-accessory production. The three men purchased the toy line and stamping dies from Streater, and Tesch immediately developed product design changes and tooling modifications.

Always one to be cautious when entering a new business venture, Crounse and Baker commissioned a study of the toy line, which would provide product direction. A number of children were surveyed, and several factors became quite clear. Children wanted toys that were sturdy and would last under harsh sandbox conditions. They also wanted the toys to actually pick up dirt or dig into the earth, and the children wanted the toys to look real. With these factors in mind, Tesch upgraded the dies for the Steam Shovel and Crane & Clam, and Mound Metalcraft had their new toy line ready for the 1947 New York Toy Show.

The new company was now underway, but capital was quickly being absorbed by start-up costs. Crounse began an intense effort to arrange additional financing, and Tesch continued to refine the company's products. The three men decided they would offer a preview of the new toy line for the 1947 toy show circuit, but they were only missing one component—a logo. To solve this problem, Lynn Baker contacted Erling W. Eklof, a resident of Mound. Eklof was a freelance industrial artist who had designed a number of logos for several companies in the Twin Cities area, and he was given the task of designing a Tonka logo in three days.

A study of Eklof's work reveals several ingenuous elements that signify the Tonka name. Eklof spoke of his work with Tonka many years later in an interview with Lloyd Lauman that explained the design of the first Tonka logo. The wave pattern that runs through the horizontal axes signifies the waters of Lake Minnetonka, and the three birds are pictured for two reasons. The first reason is that, according to Eklof, three is an odd number, which is more distinctive, and the second is that the birds represent the founders. Tonka's first label was an oval because, according to Eklof, the oval is a more recognizable shape than a square. For his work Eklof was paid a grand sum of $30.

The Mound Metalcraft Company now had several products to offer the postwar consumer market. Crounse, Baker, and Tesch felt confident in the diversity of their product line. If they couldn't make a profit from closet accessories, they might make it with garden tools. If either of those products didn't pan out, they could fall back on the toy line. The spirit and determination of the three men ultimately led to the world's largest producer of toy trucks, but first there were more hurdles to jump.

Fast Fact

Mound Metalcraft's first Tonka toy, the No. 100 Steam Shovel, was manufactured in two different color combinations for 1947. For the first few months, Tonka chose to continue with Streater Industry's colors of a black chassis with a red cab and a blue bucket and boom. Several months later, Mound Metalcraft changed the Steam Shovel to a red chassis, cab, and boom with a blue bucket and bucket arm. This change was made due to limited painting capacity and consumer input. The cab of the shovel had two oblong-shaped window openings in the front and no side cab openings. The Tonka logo appeared on the center of each side panel on the Steam Shovel's cab. The Shovel measured 16 inches long, 7 1/2 inches high, and 5 inches wide.

The second toy, the No. 150 Crane & Clam, was introduced around the same time as the Steam Shovel. The 150 used the same chassis and cab as the 100, but a crane boom and clam bucket were added. The early 1947 No. 150 had a black chassis and boom with a yellow cab and bucket. No. 150 models that came out in late 1947 had a plated bucket. The Tonka Toys logo appeared on the center of each side panel of the Crane & Clam cab. There were two control cranks on the right side of the cab. The upper crank controlled the up-and-down movement of the boom, while the lower crank raised and lowered the clam bucket. A spring-loaded lever on the left side opened and closed the clam bucket. The No. 150 Crane & Clam measured 26 inches long, 7 1/2 inches tall, and 5 inches wide.

Both the model 100 and 150 used four black rubber tires that were 1 3/4 inches in diameter and had three vertical treads. A 1947 or 1948 version of these two toys is easy to identify because of the rounded end of the chassis. The design of the chassis and cab was changed beginning in 1949.

The difference between an original Streater Industries version and a Tonka is in the decal. The Streater Industries version has only one round Streater logo decal in the rear center section of the shovel's cab.

Chapter 2

1948–1949

The start of any new manufacturing concern is never without an endless array of details, some of which must be taken care of before any products are brought to the market. Crounse, Baker, and Tesch had somewhat of an advantage in the beginning of Mound Metalcraft Company because of their extensive business contacts. Whatever knowledge they didn't possess, they were able to obtain through contacts. Whether it was talented people to operate and maintain the machines or purchasing the machines themselves, the three founders had set their course, and the late 1940s was crucial to the company's future.

The toy line purchased from Streater was ready for production by 1947. Tesch had modified the dies, but there were other hurdles to cross. One of these was the packaging for the Steam Shovel and Crane & Clam. Help came from a business contact of Lynn Baker named Mort Jamieson, who represented Waldorf Paper Products and had already supplied packaging for Mound Metalcraft's tie racks. Waldorf presented an offer for a corrugated box for the packaging of Tonka's first toy line. The new Tonka logo, designed by Erling Eklof, was prominently displayed on the sides of the box. The toys needed decals to proudly broadcast the Tonka name. Walt Erickson, who represented the Durochrome Decal Company, supplied the decals for the toys, and the line was ready for the market. The agreement between

1949 No. 100 Deluxe Steam Shovel on a No. 125 Tractor-Carry-All Trailer.
Dennis David

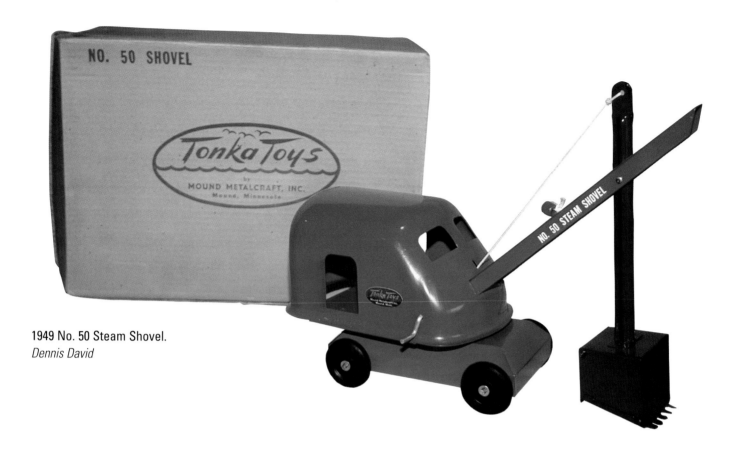

NO. 50 SHOVEL

1949 No. 50 Steam Shovel.
Dennis David

Mound Metalcraft, Waldorf Paper, and Durochrome served all three companies well, and their relationship continued for the next 20 years.

The old schoolhouse in Mound was a beehive of activity as the toy line began to take shape. The basement of the school was used as the metal-stamping and painting departments. The first floor was divided into a tool room and sub-assembly room. Company headquarters, storage, and assembly operations were located on the second floor. Mound Metalcraft employed 25 people in the beginning, and the work force was increased to 40 people (including both office and factory employees) by the end of September. The elements were now in place to propel the Tonka toy line to new highs.

The toys were introduced at the New York Toy Show and managed to generate a fair amount of enthusiasm. Sales figures for 1947 show that Mound Metalcraft's toys were just what children of the postwar era wanted. According to company records, 37,000 Steam Shovel and Crane & Clam units were built, but a quick calculation of the Mound Metalcraft's financial statements for the year does not support this claim. For 1947, gross sales are listed at $1,878.67. The sale price of the Shovel is listed at $1.90 with a suggested retail price of $3.49. The sale price of the Crane & Clam is listed at $2.16

with a suggested retail price of $3.49. If Mound Metalcraft manufactured 37,000 toys in 1947, they must have been heavily discounted or perhaps given away for promotion. Another explanation is that the fiscal year ended on June 30, 1947, and the majority of the toys were shipped between July 1947 and November 1947. Most of the 1947 sales were reflected in the $151,962.64 gross sales reported on June 30, 1948. (The fiscal year was changed to coincide with the calendar year in 1969.)

For 1948, sales took off, and a total of 79,600 units were sold. After only one year in business, Mound Metalcraft's facilities were already cramped for space, and an addition was built. The tool room was moved into the basement and the upstairs assembly floor was enlarged. This was a time of a huge demand for new products on all levels of the American consumer market. Mound Metalcraft was following the automotive industries' lead in regard to expansion and sales increases. Many auto manufacturers created new designs, and 1949 was a banner year for the American automobile. Consumers bought anything in sight, and the timing could not have been better for Mound Metalcraft's entrance into the U.S. toy market.

The first two toys solidified Tonka's reputation for durability, and it was time for the company to diversify their offerings. The first two Tonka toys proved beyond a doubt that children liked toys that moved and actually worked. Perhaps this is what led to the development of the No. 200 Lift Truck and Cart. It was a marvelous toy that simulated the heavy lifting accomplished by many primitive forklift-type machines. The very first of these toys were made from aluminum and were left unpainted on the underside. Because steel was becoming abundant once again, production was switched from aluminum to steel, but the color remained the same. The mast of the lift truck was a 1/8-inch wire form, and the lift slid up and down the mast. All of the action on the lift truck was controlled by a crank on the side that lifted the mechanism by winding a white cord around a center eyelet. Once again, Durochrome supplied a decal for the toy that completed the bold look of this new product. The decal featured two lines of gold block lettering and numbers. The Lift Truck also came with a trailer. The suggested retail price for the No. 200 Power lift was $2.49. Company records did not document the total output of the Powerlift, but former employees estimated production at about 25,000 units.

1949 No. 200 Power Lift Truck.
Lee Klancher

Russ Wenkstern

To many people who study the history of toys, Russ Wenkstern will always be known as the man who guided Tonka through many years of success, but to the employees who worked at the Mound, Minnesota, facility, he was known as "Mr. Tonka." "Wenkstern was one of those managers with a rare talent for getting along with everyone, and in turn, everyone liked him," said Lloyd Laumann, former vice president of manufacturing.

Wenkstern came from very humble beginnings. He was born in Iowa to a large family of eight children and lived on the family farm until the age of 22. He then attended college and majored in industrial arts and mathematics. He taught school for seven years and went to work in Alaska as a machinist for the Canadian/American National Oil Lease. Wenkstern spent the next year in Alaska, but then returned to the Midwest and worked for Streater Industries. Wenkstern worked for Molded Products, another toy company, and went back to Streater for a brief time before he started at Mound Metalcraft in 1952. Wenkstern rose through the ranks and eventually became president and chairman of the board of Tonka Toys.

By all accounts, Wenkstern was an interesting man. Many of the people interviewed for this book had a special story about him. He was a passionate man who was compelled to create success through the work force at Tonka. Wenkstern retired in 1977 and spent his retirement years active in his church and devoted to his passion for golf. Wenkstern owned golf courses in the Mound area, which are still in business today. Wenkstern passed away in 2000, but not before he was inducted into the Toy Manufacturers Hall of Fame. Although the Tonka name is now worldwide and has little to do with Mound, Minnesota, the name Russ Wenkstern is forever engraved in the history of the Tonka Toy Company.

Mound Metalcraft needed a toy to continue their success and penetrate even further into the toy field. Many other toy companies offered everything from cars to airplanes, and the Tonka line needed a market niche. While Mound Metalcraft certainly possessed the machinery to build any type of pressed-steel toy, it was decided that a truck would be an appropriate choice. The impetus for the truck's design would be Alvin Tesch, who simply noted the presence of a GMC cabover truck, which was parked next to the schoolhouse in the summer of 1948. There are many who believe that the first Tonka is patterned after a late 1940s Ford cabover design, but an interview with Tesch by Lloyd Lauman on May 28, 1986, confirmed he used a GMC for the new truck's prototype design.

Tesch's design of the dump truck was presented to Lynn Baker during the summer of 1948, and Baker liked the sharp and realistic look of the new toy. The tooling was designed, details were worked out, and with a lot of hard work and effort, the new truck was offered in 1949. This truck is easily identified by collectors because the one unique feature to the 1949 style is a front-wheel support bracket welded to the bottom of the chassis. This changed for the 1950 line when George Silus, a Mound Metalcraft employee, came up with a way to mount the axle by stamping a bracket from the front center section of the truck chassis. The design change saved material and reduced labor costs, but it also provided the 1949 trucks with their own identifier.

Mound Metalcraft now produced several different toys. The company's reputation for building solid and realistic toys grew every day. Gross sales exceeded $250,000 in 1949, a new record for the young company. Two more additions were built onto the old schoolhouse and allowed the company to increase production. Although it seemed that the money would pour in, the company still operated at a loss, probably because of the immense amount of capital needed for start-up and expansion. At this point, the three founders had to make a decision; they could fold and take their losses, or they could forge ahead and hope for the best. They chose to hang their hats on the success of the new truck line, which proved to be very successful. The decision to move ahead was a bold one, and Mound Metalcraft offered 13 models for 1949. The company also printed its first catalog in 1949, which described the company's offerings in detail by using color and exciting descriptions of the toys.

The 1949 Tonka Toys catalog.
Lloyd L. Laumann collection

The new catalog proudly boasted the durability of the Tonka toy line. "The Finest Quality at the Lowest Price in Metal Toys" was the slogan that carried Mound Metalcraft to success beyond anyone's imagination. The small and minor changes to the 1949 toy lineup signified what became a Tonka tradition. For 1949, the Shovel and Crane & Clam models received rubber tracks. The Steam Shovel also received a new chassis, the windows were changed to a rectangular shape, and rectangular-shaped door cutouts were added to the Shovel's cab sides for 1949. The dump truck received a decal in the front corners of each side of the dump box. The "No. 180" letters were printed in white with a transparent background. These letters disappeared in 1950, which left an original 1949 Tonka truck fairly easy to identify.

These are the types of changes that were made from year to year. At a glance, many different mod-

Profile

Doris LeGault

Doris LeGault greeted many people at the front door of Tonka's plant for many years. As the receptionist and office service coordinator, she had a front seat to all of Tonka's changes through the years. In her years with Tonka, she saw many upgrades in the phone network system. "When I started, we had a system where I had to plug and unplug jacks in order to connect callers to Tonka personnel," she said. The calls LeGault answered for Tonka were anything from business issues to family problems. "We always put family calls through to employees because we thought it was important for employee morale," LeGault said.

LeGault has many fond memories of several members of Tonka's management team throughout the years. "Charlie Groschen, Mac MacDonald, Lynn Baker, and Russ Wenkstern were all such nice people to be around," she said. She especially remembers Wenkstern and his unique ability to motivate people. "He was always good for a laugh, and there just aren't enough people like him around anymore," she said.

Through the years, LeGault has kept in touch with a few employees from Tonka, but many have moved on. Even though it's been many years since she worked there, her voice still has a sense of pride for the Tonka name. "When I see a Tonka toy on the shelf of a toy store, I look at it and think how happy I am that the name is still around. They may look a little different, but they're still a Tonka."

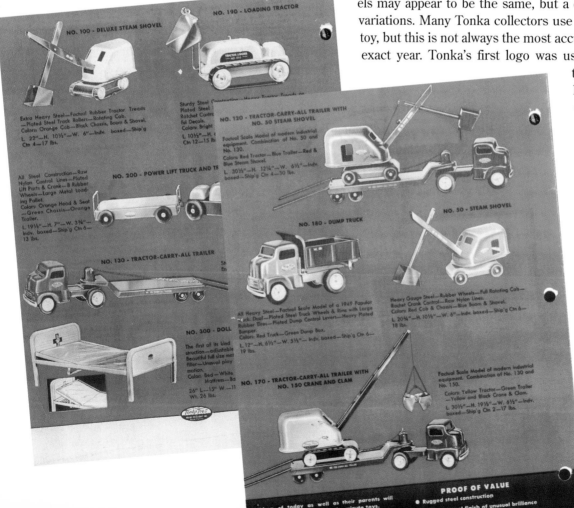

els may appear to be the same, but a close inspection will reveal minor variations. Many Tonka collectors use the decal to identify the year of a toy, but this is not always the most accurate way to positively identify the exact year. Tonka's first logo was used from its introduction in 1947 through 1955. Changes in Tonka's logo came from a collaborative effort between Tonka and Durochrome, the sole supplier for the logo. There are color variations and differences in the letters' height and width. The most accurate way to identify Tonka toys is to inspect the accessories, colors, graphics, design, and stock number.

In the late 1940s and early 1950s, Mound Metalcraft recognized the fact that girls needed toys, too. The No. 300 Doll Hospital Bed with a Mattress is a good example of Tonka's attempt to reach out to girls. The bed featured a red cross on the headboard, and the Tonka logo appeared on the footboard with the words "Doll Bed" just below the name. The doll bed was never a big seller, and very few were made. Former Tonka employees estimated that less than 2,000 were ever built, and the bed was discontinued after 1950.

Variations were made to the product line, thanks to simple ingenuity. The 1949 catalog features the Tractor-Carry-All Trailer. This toy combined some of Tonka's existing products with a new trailer. The No. 130 Carry-All used the truck cab and chassis and added a trailer that carried the No. 100 Steam Shovel. This impressive toy measured 30 1/2 inches long. Another variation is the No.190 Loading Tractor, which used the same tooling as the No. 200 Powerlift but with a scoop and tracks. This toy was only manufactured in 1949. Former employees and collectors seldom locate this unique toy.

The bold marketing and impressive toys of the 1949 lineup proved that the Tonka name stood for quality and durability. Crounse, Baker, and Tesch had come a long way since 1946. In just three years, they had managed to create a name that children everywhere could identify.

The 1949 toy line sold record numbers, and it was time for Mound Metalcraft to assume its position as a leader in the toy industry. The plans for the garden tools and closet accessories were discarded, and Mound Metalcraft focused exclusively on its toy line. One could say that the company was now on firm ground and the future appeared bright. America itself was still prospering, and the decade of the wonderful 1950s was just around the corner. America was about to enter an era of prosperity that it had never seen before. Tonka became the toy of choice for children all over the nation, and the little schoolhouse in Mound, Minnesota, stood ready to deliver.

The 1949 Tonka Toys catalog.
Lloyd L. Laumann collection

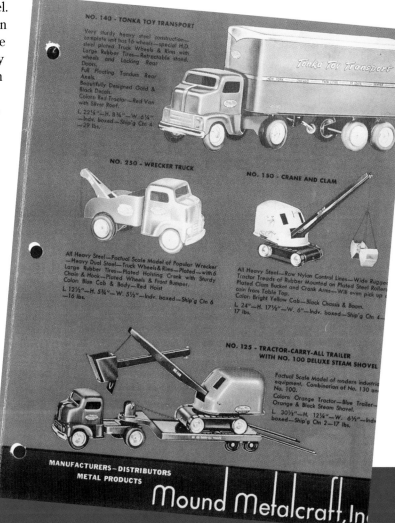

Fast Fact

Tonka offered 13 toys in 1949. The No. 130 Carry-All, No. 140 Tonka Toy Transport, No. 180 Dump Truck, and the No. 250 Wrecker all used the same cab, patterned after a GMC cabover. The three toys originally offered previous to 1949 were also carried over, but the stock numbers were changed. The No. 100 Shovel became No. 50 and was virtually identical except for a color change. The No. 150 Crane & Clam received rubber tracks for 1949, and the No. 200 Powerlift's name was changed to Power Lift Truck and Trailer.

The remaining four models from 1949 included the No. 100 Deluxe Steam Shovel, No. 120 Carry-All Trailer with No. 50 Steam Shovel, No. 125 Carry-All Trailer with No. 100 Deluxe Steam Shovel, and No. 170 Carry-All Trailer with No. 150 Clam.

Chapter 3

1950–1952

By 1950, Tonka had established itself as a recognized brand name in the American toy market. Mound Metalcraft joined the Toy Manufacturers of America (TMA), and consumers everywhere associated the Tonka name with a durable toy that offered many hours of fun. The old schoolhouse in Mound had been enlarged for a third time, but the company still didn't have enough space. William H. A. Koehler lived next door to the school and sold his home to the company. This two-story home became the new corporate offices of Mound Metalcraft Incorporated.

Production exceeded sales for 1949; therefore, some of the finished product inventory was carried over for 1950. The entire lineup from 1949 was offered, and Tonka introduced four new models to help Tonka penetrate the market even further.

The 1950 product line offered the new No. 145 Steel Carrier, which spoke of Tonka's realism and prototypical accuracy. The truck was accurately proportioned and used 10 tires to simulate a heavy-duty truck that could haul steel. Tonka used bold colors on the truck—the trailer carrier was painted green with yellow decals, and the tractor was orange. At a length of 22 inches, it is an impressive toy that commands a handsome price in today's collector market.

1952 No. 145 Steel Carrier.
Dennis David

1950 No. 185 Tonka Express.
Lee Klancher

The No. 185 Tonka Express Truck debuted in 1950 and was basically a box truck with a dual rear axle that was painted red and green. The Express was only offered for one year before it was retired. There was also a No. 175 Utility Hauler that was similar to the Express Truck but had a stake-bed body. The Tonka Doll Bed was also updated and offered again for 1950. The updated version (No. 310 Doll Bed) carried the same basic style, but it was finished in Metallic Blue. As with the original version, the updated version sold poorly. Although the company tried to diversify its product line, Tonka quickly became known as a line of sturdy trucks, and this was the hallmark of Mound Metalcraft Inc. for many years.

With Tonka's reputation for well-built toys at affordable prices reaching new levels of market penetration every day, the stage was set for Mound Metalcraft to dominate the U.S. toy truck market in the 1950s. There were other toy companies, but none experienced the growth and market share that Tonka was accumulating. In particular, Buddy L enjoyed the expanding U.S. toy market in the early 1950s and was Tonka's closest competitor for several years. Buddy L supplied war materials to the government in the early 1940s but also managed to market a few wooden toys during those years. Originally established in 1921 as a manufacturer of car parts, Buddy L switched over to children's toys after the success of a few custom trucks, which were built by founder Fred Lundahl for his son, Buddy, for whom the company was named. Buddy L's postwar market success can be attributed to many of the same tactics used by Tonka, which were virtually indestructible toys that looked real and withstood the harsh elements of the sandbox.

The Nylint Company was also on the forefront of the American toy market. David Nyberg and Bernard C. Klint (hence the name Nylint) founded the company in 1937 and began by manufacturing realistic, rugged construction toys. After World War II, Nylint moved into trucks with great success, and it enjoys that same success today.

Another company, Smith-Miller, was founded in 1945 and manufactured toy trucks that had a high degree of detail and realism that is still highly respected. Smith-Miller closed its doors in 1954 as the market became saturated, but toys from "Smitty" are highly collectible and command high prices at auctions everywhere.

In the face of such strong competition, Mound Metalcraft decided to refocus its sales strategy for 1951, and a new marketing plan was implemented. The number of models in the line was reduced. This helped streamline production, control costs, and improve delivery time. This move also allowed the company more time to work on specials and private label and promotional toys.

Prior to 1951, Mound Metalcraft's manufacturing departments were idle from late November to late March. For 1951, the plant was open from January through the first week of December. This strategy worked well for Tonka, and by March 31, 1951, Tonka had completed 16.5 percent of its annual production. Mound Metalcraft showed its first profit, and gross sales were $361,204. The new sales strategies were working, and the Tonka name was growing by the day.

The year 1951 marked the introduction of a truck from Tonka that became a staple in the line for many decades. The Allied Van was available in several different configurations and survived many models changes. The very first Allied Van was designed by Charles M. Groschen, who worked for the Markson Company during the day and for Tonka at night. Groschen designed many more toys for Tonka, and his name became synonymous with Tonka's place in history, but the Allied Van has a story all its own.

Groschen designed the first Allied Van according to exact specifications. The early Tonka Allied Vans have a realistic look that is seldom matched in the toy market. Groschen was able to copy the exact specifications from Allied Van, thanks to an agreement between Allied and Tonka. Groschen designed the first Allied Van for the 1951 Toy Fair, which company president Lynn Baker personally took to the show.

No. 120 - TRACTOR-CARRY-ALL TRAILER WITH No. 50 STEAM SHOVEL

Factual Scale Model of modern industrial equipment. Combination of No. 50 and No. 130.

Colors: Red Tractor—Blue Trailer—Red & Blue Steam Shovel.

L. 30½"—H. 12¼"—W. 6½"—Individually boxed—Shipping Carton 3—23 lbs.

No. 250 - WRECKER TRUCK

All Heavy Steel—Factual Scale Model of Popular Wrecker—Heavy Dual Steel—Truck Wheels & Rims—Plated—with 6 Large Rubber Tires—Plated Hoisting Crank with Sturdy Chain & Hook—Plated Wheels & Front Bumper.

Color: Blue Cab & Body—Red Hoist.

L. 12½"—H. 5¾"—W. 5½"—Individually boxed—Shipping Carton 6—16 lbs.

No. 400 "ALLIED" VAN

An "Exclusive" Authorized Reproduction in miniature of Allied Van Lines recommended Equipment for their Agents.

Heavy steel construction - with Retractable stand wheels and Locking Rear Doors.

Ten Big Rubber Truck Tires Mounted on Plated Steel Truck Wheels.

Baked on Enamel Finish with standard "Allied" Decals.

Color: "Omaha" Orange

L. 23-½"—H. 8-½"—W. 5-¾"—Individually Boxed—Shipping Carton 4—Wt. 22 lbs.

NOTE: We reserve the right to make substitutions in materials without prior notice.

1952 Tonka Toys catalog.
Lloyd L. Laumann collection

Profile
Fran Murphy

Fran Murphy began working at Tonka in 1952 and stayed with the company for 27 years. Although she originally applied to work in the administrative office, she was told at the interview that office help was not needed, but they could find a place for her on the factory floor. "I put pieces and parts together, but I was learning the toy business," she said. After about six months on the job, Gordon Batdorf said there was a job opening in the office. After a brief typing test, she was given a job as Lynn Baker's secretary. "I remember being nervous about the whole thing," Fran said, "but Lynn and I had a talk and he said that we would get along just fine, and we did." Fran enjoyed working for Lynn Baker very much.

Fran's major contribution to Tonka in those early years is that she set up the filing system that tracked Mound Metalcraft's cash flow and production. "It was very hectic in those days because the company was always living on borrowed money," Fran said. She was also in charge of Tonka's Toy Donation Program, which began in 1953. Through the program, hundreds of children that otherwise would not have toys received Tonka toys. The program was a great success and demonstrated the spirit of Tonka's employees. "When I look back on my years at Tonka, I think that my fondest memories are of the Donation Program," she said.

Like most former employees, Fran's heart was broken when Tonka left Mound. "I've never gotten over the fact that they're gone. Our office was like one big happy family, and it was a fun place to work." Fran retired in 1979 and has spent her retirement years in Minnesota a few miles from where she used to work. "Tonka was a big part of my life, and I could never leave the area that holds so many wonderful memories for me."

Tonka logo from 1947 to 1955.
Lee Klancher

The introduction of the Allied Van marked a 30-year agreement between Tonka and Allied. An Allied Van can be found in Tonka's yearly offerings, from the very early styles to the mini Tonka private-label Allied Van of 1981. Tracing the Allied Van from Tonka is like chronicling the company's styles over many years. The Allied Van also marked the beginning of a specialty line for Tonka that was very profitable. Gambles Department Stores, G. Fox & Co., Carnation Milk, Ace Hardware, Jewel Tea Company, Hormel, Marshall Field & Company, and United Van Lines are a few of the specialty Tonkas that were offered.

The early 1950s were good years for Tonka. The company was on firm financial ground and manufactured toys by the thousands, but this created a few problems on its own. Tonka had various parts left over from a production run, and there was no desire to just throw them away. Tonka created a policy to use up older parts whenever possible to finish up a production run. The company substituted wheels, decals, headlights, grilles, chains, and colors to complete a production run. Company policy provided that this was an acceptable practice as long as the parts were only used from the previous year. This policy created inconsistencies within the Tonka product line in any given year. Tonka collectors who try to match a specific model to a catalog photo may find that a Tonka toy from this era does not completely match the catalog. This practice continued until 1966, when Tonka began shipping obsolete parts to Rayon Surfaces Limited in Auckland, New Zealand. Rayon used the leftover parts to assemble a line of toys that were similar to Tonka's, and these toys usually have identifiers stating they were made in New Zealand.

Tonka also experienced another first with the 1952 line. A small catalog was packed inside each box. The small catalog did not contain the full detail of the larger catalog, but it did give

1952 Tonka Toys catalog.
Lloyd L. Laumann collection

GENERAL OFFICES of Tonka Toys, Inc., are located in the building above, located on a hill next to Plant No. 1.

General offices of Tonka Toys Inc.
Lloyd L. Laumann collection

buyers a look at the company's other offerings, which contributed to more sales. Collectors run across these catalogs from time to time, but they usually are in poor condition.

Along with success and growth, the usual growing pains associated with any successful business happened when Mound Metalcraft encountered one of its first controversies in 1952. Moving production from the old schoolhouse in Mound to a new facility in Tennessee was considered. With Mound Metalcraft clearly on its way to becoming a major manufacturer in the industrial landscape, the state of Tennessee began courting the company with generous tax incentives and a financially attractive 10-year lease on a building that guaranteed ownership of the facility at the end of the lease. Crounse and Tesch were in favor of the move, but Lynn Baker stood fast and maintained that the Tonka name was engrained in the Mound,

No. 175 · UTILITY HAULER
Latest in design and styling—Heavy gauge construction—Embossed stakes on side panels—Dual Wheels—6 Large Rubber Tires—Plated Steel Rims—High gloss Baked Enamel Finish.
Colors: Orange Truck—Green Body.
L. 12"—H. 5¾"—W. 5½"—Individually boxed—Shipping Carton 6—17 lbs.

No. 550 · GRAIN HAULER
Scale Model of One of the Most Popular Styles of Tractor-Trailer Units Today. Rolled Edges on Trailer Body with Rugged Embossed Steel Sides—Tandem Rear Axle—14 Large Truck Tires on Plated Steel Wheels—Retractable Stand Wheels.
Color: Plated Trailer Body—Red Tractor
L. 22¼"—H. 5¾"—W. 5¾"
Individually Boxed—Shipped 4 per Bundle—20 Pounds.

No. 50 · STEAM SHOVEL
Heavy Gauge Steel—Rubber Wheels—Full Rotating Cab—Ratchet Crank Control—Raw Nylon Lines.
Colors: Red Cab & Chassis—Blue Boom & Shovel.
L. 20¾"—H.10½"—W. 6"—Individually boxed—Shipping Carton 6—18 lbs.

No. 145 · STEEL CARRIER
Factual Scale Model Carrier with Rolled Edges—Dual Wheels—Plated Steel Rims—10 Large Rubber Tires—Fifth Wheel Device for Coupling and Uncoupling Tractor and Carrier. Retractable Stand Wheels.
Colors: Orange Tractor—Green Carrier—Yellow Decals.
L. 22"—H. 5¾"—W. 5¾"—Individually boxed—Shipping Carton 4—22 lbs.

NO. 500 LIVE STOCK VAN
The "First" Actual Scale Model of America's Most Popular Farm Truck. Unusual Appeal for Both Adult and Child—Top Rated Play Value—Heavy Steel Construction—Plus 14 H. D. Truck Tires on Plated Steel Wheels—Retractable Stand Wheels—Tandem Rear Axle.
Color: Popular "Farm" Red.
L. 22¼" H. 9¼" W. 6¼".
Individually Boxed—Shipped 4 per Bundle—28#

No. 180 · DUMP TRUCK
All Heavy Steel—Factual Scale Model of a 1950 Popular Truck. Dual—Plated Steel Truck Wheels & Rims with Large Rubber Tires — Plated Dump Control Levers — Heavy Plated Bumper.
Colors: Red Truck—Green Dump Box.
L. 12"—H. 6½"—W. 5½"—Individually boxed—Shipping Carton 6—19 lbs.

No. 140 · TONKA TOY TRANSPORT
Very sturdy heavy steel construction—complete unit has 16 wheels—special H.D. steel plated Truck Wheels & Rims with Large Rubber Tires—Retractable standwheels and Locking Rear Doors.
Full Floating Tandem Rear Axles.
Beautifully Designed Gold & Black Decals.
Colors: Red Tractor—Red Van.
L. 22¼"—H. 8¾"—W. 6¼"—Individually boxed—Shipping Carton 4—29 lbs.

MOUND METALCRAFT, Inc., Mound, Minnesota

1952 Tonka Toys catalog.
Lloyd L. Laumann collection

Profile
Verna Gutzke

Verna Gutzke remembers her years at Tonka like they were yesterday. She started working for Tonka in the old schoolhouse in October 1953. Hired as an assembler, she moved into inspection and ultimately wound up as a group leader. "I remember the day we were making the red-and-green dump trucks and a new rivet machine came in. We needed another one because business was going well." She also applied a lot of decals and assembled many different Tonka products over the years. She estimates that she handled hundreds of thousands of toys in her years at Tonka.

Gutzke experienced a lot of changes as Tonka grew through the years. "I remember that wheels were dumped into a little chute, and we would put them on one at a time," she said. In later years, automated machines were used to attach thousands of wheels per day without a single human hand touching the toy.

Gutzke still has fond memories of working at the old schoolhouse. "I remember that we would always play tricks on each other." One of them was when someone was in the elevator that ran between the three floors, someone would open a door halfway, trip the safety switch, and lock the person in the elevator until they screamed loud enough to be heard. "There was also a bakery on the back side of the schoolhouse, and we would run out on our break and get a fresh roll," Gutzke said. Working at Tonka really was a family affair for Gutzke—her mother worked there and her husband was a materials handler for 30 years.

Life is simpler for Gutzke now as she enjoys her retirement years, but she looks back on her years at Tonka with a sense of pride and commitment. "It really was fun working there, and they really did employ the best people in the world."

Minnesota, landscape. The proposed move also brought other issues to light–it revealed philosophical differences, and Crounse and Tesch sold their interests in Mound Metalcraft and moved on. While the departure of two of the founding members left a cloud of uncertainty over the company, the door was now open for new blood and fresh ideas.

Lynn Baker suffered a heart attack on August 7, 1949, and by 1952, he decreased his workload. In order to continue to build Tonka into a world-recognized brand name, he had to be very careful about who he selected to lead the company. He chose Gordon E. Batdorf to be his vice president and treasurer. Batdorf had joined Mound

DUMP TRUCK   No. 180

Factual scale model. Heavy steel dual rear wheels. Rubber tires.
L. 12"—H. 6½"—W. 5½"

No. 145   **STEEL CARRIER**

Accurate scale model. rubber tires. Both tractor a trailer have dual whee Retractable stand wheels.
L. 22"—H. 5¾"—W. 5¾'

No. 500   **LIVESTOCK VAN**

"A First" in a miniature scale model of America's most popular farm truck. Unusual appeal for both adult and child—top rated play value. Truck tires on plated steel wheels. Full-floating tandem axle on trailer. Locking stand wheels.
L. 22½"—H. 9¼"—W. 6¼"

A miniature catalog from 1952.
Lloyd L. Laumann collection

Metalcraft in 1947 after serving in the U.S. Air Force as a fighter pilot. He returned from the war a decorated war hero and sought peacetime employment in Mound. Batdorf was originally hired as the company's bookkeeper, and he worked his way up the company ladder. He was the board of directors' secretary from 1949 to 1952.

For the rest of Tonka's leading team, Baker hired Russell L. Wenkstern, who was crucial to Tonka's future. After he was appointed as secretary on January 21, 1952, Wenkstern led Mound Metalcraft to new highs. Wenkstern was initially hired as plant superintendent and led Tonka in many other positions for the next 25 years. Wenkstern was a former high-school shop teacher who had six years of manufacturing experience with Molded Products and Streater Industries. Lynn Baker certainly knew potential when he saw it, and it has been said by many that he saw the future of Tonka in Wenkstern.

With the departure of Crounse and Tesch, Lynn Baker held 60 percent of Mound Metalcraft's common stock, and Batdorf and Wenkstern each held a respectable 15 percent, with the remainder held by M. H. McDonald, Florence L. Baker (Lynn's wife), and the treasury. The elements were now in place to put Mound Metalcraft into a very profitable decade.

Russell L. Wenkstern.
Lloyd L. Laumann collection

Fast Fact

By the middle of 1952, Mound Metalcraft's total number of employees had reached 75 people. Production scheduling mandated that the company was closed for only one month during late December and early January. Total production for the calendar year equaled $595,170, and sales amounted to $594,154. Business picked up in the latter half of 1952, and the company shipped $40,762 worth of products during December alone. The year 1952 was Mound Metalcraft's second profitable year in a row.

With the new management team in place, a new era of enthusiasm took hold at Mound Metalcraft. The employees were recognized as the company's most important asset, and they responded with good morale and high productivity. Management encouraged employee involvement in the company and was ready and willing to listen to any and all of the employees' concerns. Tonka employee Bill Dressel received a check for $100 for suggesting that Tonka build a livestock van. George Silus, another employee, was featured in a newspaper ad announcing his promotion to tool-and-die shop foreman. Silus also cochaired the first annual Tonka picnic to which all employees and their families were invited. Mound Metalcraft was developing a good employee base that was the foundation for its modern-day success.

The No. 500 Livestock Van and the No. 550 Grain Hauler were two new models introduced in 1952. One of the first Tonka toys, the No. 150 Crane & Clam, was dropped from the lineup that same year. It reappeared in several different forms and became a staple in the Tonka lineup, but the original style never saw production again. For collectors of minute Tonka detail, there is a mistake in the 1952 catalog. The catalog states that the trailer body and door on the No. 550 Grain Hauler are made from embossed steel. The components were actually manufactured out of aluminum, but records do not indicate if anyone from the general public was aware of the inconsistency. Nowadays such a mistake would invoke the wrath of several consumer groups, but then America was set in a decade of innocence, and children playing with their Tonka Toy trucks didn't care if they were made from steel or aluminum.

Chapter 4

1953–1955

THE SUCCESS OF THE TONKA TOY LINE IN THE 1950S EXCEEDED EVERYONE'S WILDEST DREAMS. THE old schoolhouse in Mound operated at near-maximum capacity, and the philosophy of the company managers and directors created a work environment that was productive and comfortable. Several former employees of the Mound plant said the primary reason for the good morale at Tonka was based solely on the fact that they made toys. "It's not like we were building kitchen appliances or parts for a machine that most of the world would never see. We were building toys for kids, and most of us at the plant had kids, so we genuinely cared about our products," said Fran Murphy, an employee for 27 years. Whatever the reason, Tonka was on its way to dominate the U.S. toy truck market.

For 1953, sales exceeded $1 million. A grand total of $1,277,740 was generated in sales, and production equaled $1,275,714. Profits totaled $11,593, but despite the small profit, Tonka was still Mound's largest manufacturer. Tonka's marketing department completed a nationwide analysis in the mid-1970s that revealed interesting trends that developed during those formative years of the 1950s and into the 1970s. During the 20-year span from 1953 to 1973, the states of Connecticut, Delaware, Maryland, New Jersey, New York, Pennsylvania, and Washington, D.C., accounted for 35 to 40 percent of all Tonka sales. California accounted for

1954 No. 175-4 Utility Truck.
Dennis David

12 percent, and Texas stood at 8 percent. This means that more than half of Tonka's annual production volume was sold in these eight states and Washington, D.C. The possibility exists that distribution to these areas was better than in the other states, but Tonka's saturation of the toy market in the coming years reached to all of the other states.

With business booming, Tonka expanded its product line for 1953 with a grand total of 14 models. This was also a big year for design changes and an introduction of several new models that solidified Tonka's position in the toy truck market. A new Road Grader appeared in 1953, and this toy alone would stay with Tonka in one form or another until 1991. Tonka's Road Grader was produced for 38 years. In modern manufacturing terms, this is an incredible amount of time for a product to stay in production. Hasbro continued manufacturing the original design into the new millennium.

Feature Road Grader.
Lee Klancher

Perhaps the reason for the Road Grader's success was its dedication to realism. It had the ability to adjust and tilt the grader blade, and movable steering enabled it to go where needed. The standard Tonka wheel was nothing like a real road grader would use, so a new tire was designed and the sole supplier was the Nye Rubber Company of Barberton, Ohio. It was a solid wheel that featured a 2 3/4-inch V-grip tread that looked real. This tire was used on Tonka's Road Graders until 1966. Tonka introduced a new hubcap on the grader that featured five round holes. Promotional material from Tonka on the 1953 product line shows a hubcap with six holes, but by the time it went into actual production, the hubcap had five holes.

Work on the Road Grader actually started in 1951 when Al Tesch started some preliminary design work, but the project was finished by Charlie Groschen, who put the finishing

Al Hilk (background), Leonard Gutzke(foreground),and an unidentified Janney Semple Hill driver load a trailer in 1954.
Lloyd L. Laumann collection

touches on it in time for the 1953 production run. Many collectors have asked where the model for the grader came from, and the answer is simple. Tesch and Groshen used a grader owned by the Cox Brothers Construction Company of Spring Park, Minnesota, as inspiration.

The year 1954 saw an increase in business that caught many Tonka employees and executives by surprise. Sales doubled from the previous year to $2,437,018, and Tonka employed 325 people. Records indicate that Lynn Baker, the president of Mound Metalcraft Inc., received a salary of $15,570 in 1954. In today's terms, this figure amounts to about $300,000.

All of Mound Metalcraft's success and expansion did not go unnoticed by the city of Mound, and the shakeup of Tonka's management in 1952 had given the city some cause for concern. After all, with Tonka's growth and subsequent hiring of many local people, city officials did not want Tonka to relocate. The Mound Chamber of Commerce recognized this concern and formed Greater Mound Inc. to keep and bring industry to Mound. They immediately purchased six acres of property to assist Mound Metalcraft with its expansion plans.

In terms of design, 1954 was a big year for Tonka as the company kept up with the changing look of the American truck. A whole new design greeted Tonka children, and the design turned out to be a huge success because everything was new. The cab, chassis, grille, and tires were all changed, and metal headlights were added to all trucks. The general look of Tonka's truck in 1954 followed styling from the Ford Motor Company with its standard and deluxe cabs. Mound Metalcraft set up the dies in the press room to punch out the new truck cab and chassis. The process of creating the new truck was not complicated, but it required an extensive amount of time due to the complicated body. Starting from flat sheet metal, the process required seven die hits. Metalcraft's presses ran 24 hours a day, five days a week to keep up. The bumper and

1953 Dump Truck.
Dennis David

Profile
Charles M. Groschen

Every product in the world has to start with a design, and at Tonka, that design started with Charles M. Groschen. Groschen started working at Tonka in 1954, but he had been designing prototype toys for Mound Metalcraft since its very beginning. From his small metal shop set up in the basement of his home, Groschen designed and built many of Tonka's prototypes. "If they wanted to build a certain model toy, I built the working prototype from scratch," Groschen said. When Tonka formally hired Groschen in 1954, his official title was Assistant Plant Manager in charge of Research and Development. Groschen also took his talents one step further and participated in the design and completion of the tooling that would make the actual toy. As opposed to a designer working in Detroit's automobile industry who only gets to design a door handle or a fender, Groschen designed the entire vehicle.

Groschen said there were many challenges in designing and building Tonka Toys due to their prototypical realism. "When you build a unit like Tonka's Road Grader as a toy, you don't have the hydraulics to make the parts move, and you have to come up with different methods of force and power. The biggest challenge is coming up with a design that looks and works like a real one but can also be produced in mass quantities at the plant," Groschen said. His inspiration for his work came from his extraordinary talent for working with sheet metal, which he had used even before Mound Metalcraft with Streater Industries. Groschen designed the original tooling for Streater Industries Steam Shovel and Crane & Clam that was purchased by Mound Metalcraft.

Groschen enjoyed his years working with all of the people from the top management to the entire work force. Groschen explained that Tonka's employees were from all over the Mound area, which was primarily farm country. "People who work on farms tend to be smart people who are able to work things out by themselves," he said. "These were proud, hardworking people that would not allow imperfect products to leave the factory."

Groschen has since retired to a warmer climate than the Minnesota winter offers, but he summed up our interview by talking about his fellow employees. "The people were what made Tonka what it really was. If we had to stay up all night to get a job ready for production, that's what we did." As for his prototype work at Tonka, Groschen said, "I wish I had kept some of those original designs—they'd probably be worth a fortune by now!"

Charles M. Groschen.
Lloyd L. Laumann collection

grille were stamped as a one-piece unit, and in the interest of simplicity and versatility, the new chassis was able to accommodate dual rear wheels and saddle fuel tanks with a fifth wheel for Tonka's semitruck line. An inspection of Tonka's trucks from this era reveals a simple design that snaps together and holds up well over the years. A hubcap may be missing, but rarely are the trucks ever missing a roof, wheel, or axle. Rigid standards and fine craftsmanship dictated that the average Tonka truck would last longer than a real truck, and to this end, many have. Tonka toys were always available at garage sales years after they were manufactured and subjected to many hours to play. It's a great testimonial to their quality.

For 1954, Tonka changed their tire design for the entire line, and the Nye Rubber Company supplied all of Tonka's tires. All of Tonka's trucks received the new hubcap that debuted on the road grader the year before. A slight change was made in the die for the 1955 truck that is hardly noticeable, but it's invaluable in identifying the two years. There is a slightly flared panel below the door on the 1955 models, and it is the only way to tell the two years apart for some models.

Tonka entered a new realm of realism with the introduction of their first fire truck in 1954. Fire trucks have always held a certain degree of fascination for any child, and Mound Metalcraft went to great lengths to create a fire truck that would make any child happy on Christmas morning. The design for the 1954 Aerial Ladder Truck was created by Charlie Groschen, who had been instrumental in many of Tonka's successful designs. The design was copied from a Minneapolis Fire Department aerial ladder truck that was manufactured by the Peter Pirsch Company of Kenosha, Wisconsin. The aerial ladder truck featured two 19-inch-long auxiliary ladders that were made from aluminum. The trailer portion of the truck carried four fire extinguishers, but it didn't have the turn wheel as it did in later models. A cone-shaped flasher was mounted on the cab roof, and there was no siren on the fender as there was on later models.

Decals for the new fire truck were works of art, as the bright gold lettering was bordered in black. The letters "M.F.D.," to represent the Mound Fire Department, were used until they were changed to "T.F.D." to stand for Tonka Fire Department. In keeping with Tonka's goal of creating realistic toys, the ladder could be raised and extended to rescue helpless victims of large building fires. The string and turnbuckle mechanism that operates the ladder portion is an ingenious design that is both functional and reliable, but it has given many restorers several opportunities to rub their chins when reconstructing the mechanism.

The International Metro Van also made its debut in 1954. Bright yellow decals that said "Parcel Delivery" in capital letters enabled many children to make imaginary deliveries all over the house. The Delivery Van had some unusual details for a Tonka. The proud Tonka decal was placed on the front fenders, and another logo appeared on the underside of the van. The van also had door handles on its side entrance door and each of its rear doors. The grille was painted to match the body color, but the bumpers were plated, and two plated buttons were used as headlights. Strangely enough, the Tonka Parcel Delivery Van was dropped in 1955 and 1956, but it reappeared in 1957 with very minor changes. Tonka sold the same style of van as a Carnation Milk Truck and a rescue van in 1955 and 1956.

Tonka's success in the early years was a direct reflection of the efforts of its employees. One of those employees was M. H. "Mac" McDonald. Mac helped make Tonka a household word in the 1950s. McDonald's official title was superintendent of maintenance, new operations, and installations. He came to Mound Metalcraft after his employer, the Industrial Tool & Die Company of Minneapolis, went out of business. To say he was very talented is an understatement. McDonald was an electrical, mechanical, and civil engineer. He had experience as a mine operator, surveyor, and tool-and-die manufacturer. McDonald's dedication to his work was so extreme that he had a bed in the attic of the old schoolhouse that he

Parcel delivery truck.
Lee Klancher

Profile
Lee Pfeilstricker

In 1954, Lee Pfeilstricker was looking for a job, and as a toolmaker, he found one at Mound Metalcraft. Lee worked directly for Charles Groschen and did all of the design work directed by Groschen. While today's design world may consist of automated machines and computer-aided drafting software programs, Pfeilstricker's design world was somewhat different. "When I started at the school-house in Mound, I had an 8-foot sheet-metal brake, a vise, tin snips, and a hammer," he said. "It was very simple back then. Charlie Groschen would tell me what they were looking for, and I would build it." Lee still has a few of the prototype designs that he built for Tonka, but over the years he has sold most of them.

According to Pfeilstricker, Tonka's strength was its people. "We employed mostly women from the surrounding farms, and they were the best workers in the world." He also knew that when the company left Mound in 1983 and headed for Mexico there would be trouble. "I felt they were wrong in making that move, because I knew they wouldn't be able to match the work force that we had in Mound," he said.

Pfeilstricker's fondest memories of his years at Tonka are the employee parties. "Sometimes we had to work 80 hours per week just before the big toy fairs, and the company would reward us after by taking us on a trip." Lee remembers one such party when they were taken on a train that provided dinner and entertainment from Mound to Hutchinson, Minnesota. Other parties involved entertainment and dining at the Lafayette Club and several dinner-theater parties in the area. "They treated us well, and it was a great place to work," he said.

Pfeilstricker still looks for Tonka's toys when he visits a toy store and notes the differences between the work he did and the work done today. "Back then we were really big on having the metal parts protect the plastic. In other words, we always placed plastic parts on the inside because it was a softer material," he said. Today's modern plastics have evolved into a very durable material, and many of Tonka's present-day toy trucks feature plastic exterior parts, something that couldn't have been done back then.

Pfeilstricker still lives on a Minnesota lake, and like so many other Tonka employees, he chose to stay in the area. Remembering his days at Tonka, he said, "It was a great place to work, and I enjoyed my years there."

would frequently use for overnight stays when he was intensely involved in new production equipment installations.

By 1955, Tonka's board of directors consisted of Baker, Batdorf, McDonald, and Wenkstern. Decades later, many people ask how a new Tonka product came to market, or who actually decided what type of model toy truck or construction vehicle would be built. The answers to these questions lie with the planning and product design evaluation committee, which consisted of six executives from the company—Lynn Baker, president; Gordon Batdorf, vice president and treasurer; Russ Wenkstern, secretary and

Tonka's second plant in Mound, Minnesota, taken in August 1955.
Lloyd L. Laumann collection

plant superintendent; T. G. Ted Shaefer, sales manager; Mac McDonald, superintendent of maintenance; and Charles M. Groschen, assistant production manager. Together, these men determined if a product had enough appeal to create the dies, devise a marketing plan, and bring the toy to consumers. History suggests they were very good at selecting the types of vehicles that children wanted in their sandbox.

The selection committee picked 22 toys to market for 1955, and expansion at the Mound facility was ongoing. Construction on the second plant began in the spring of 1955, which became the main plant for Mound Metalcraft's operations.

1954 Star Kist Tuna.
Dennis David

Fast Fact

The new plant built by Tonka in 1955 gave rise to several refinements in the construction process of the new toys. Along with the new building came a new electrostatic painting system that was state of the art for 1955. Built by Ransburg, this new system allowed Tonka to gain a brighter and more durable finish on their products. The toy parts were dipped in paint tanks and hand-sprayed; then they received a finish coat of paint in the electrostatic spray unit and were baked for a hard and durable finish. Tonka and Dupont worked closely together to perfect the new system, and together they overcame the problem of applying wet paint over wet paint without fear of runs or inconsistencies. The new process necessitated holes in the parts so they could be hung from a hook for painting. This is why there are holes in various odd places on Tonka products. On a Tonka dump truck, the hole is usually found on the dirt guard attached to the dump box that hangs over the cab roof. Other trucks were hooked through a chassis, grille, or headlight hole in order to properly paint the product. The process itself was not perfect, but it made Tonka's paint better than the competitors'. Collectors can usually distinguish between a restored and an original truck because an original might have a paint drip on the corner of the truck cab or a small run in the paint that may have occurred before drying. There also may be small inconsistencies in color because the paint dip tanks were constantly being replenished. This was simply a matter of adding more paint, and sometimes paint thinner, to maintain the proper viscosity. Tonka's new paint system for 1955 was unique, but there were no computers and it relied solely on workers. The process worked and allowed Tonka to achieve the desired results.

Chapter 5

1955–1958

Mound Metalcraft's new plant was ready in late July 1955, and production at the new facility began immediately. With employment now at 355 workers and with increasing sales, Mound Metalcraft began to operate some of its departments 24 hours a day. In an effort to gain national recognition, Mound Metalcraft president Lynn Baker sent a beautiful 1955 Aerial Ladder Truck to President Dwight D. Eisenhower's grandson, David. President Eisenhower acknowledged receipt of the fire truck in a letter to Baker.

Ever mindful of changing their toys to make them look more realistic, Tonka's Aerial Ladder Truck underwent a few alterations for 1955. A simulated die-cast siren was mounted on the right front fender of the cab, and two different flasher assemblies were used on the roof of the truck. Depending on availability, a cone- or dome-shaped flasher was mounted on the truck's roof. The four fire extinguishers were also changed for 1955 with a detailed simulated turn handle located on the top. The decal was altered, and an artistic scroll design was added just below the number "5" on the truck door. The scroll design was also added to the saddle fuel tanks on the truck, and the same artwork also appeared on the running board sides of the ladder unit.

1958 Gasoline Truck.
Dennis David

Left to right: Gert Ogitziak,
Agnes Stoltman, and Lynn E. Baker
with the 1955 Sand loader set.
Lloyd L. Laumann collection

A very unusual toy, the No. 800-5 Aerial Sand Loader, made its debut at the 1955 New York Toy Fair. Realistic features were the appeal of this toy as it was modeled from the overhead loaders used on the Lake Superior ore docks in northern Minnesota. The loader was designed to pick up and handle small rocks, pebbles, and marbles. Design work began on this loader in 1952, but the cost of steel and the intense labor involved prohibited production at that time. Steel was substituted with aluminum, and the loader was ready for production. It was sold along with Tonka's No. 180-5 Dump Truck, but the set is rarely found intact because of its many parts. It was a toy with a complex chain system that could easily be misplaced or malfunction. Tonka collectors have paid handsomely to add one of these in good condition to their collection.

Another debut was made in 1955 with Tonka's first Ford-style pickup truck. It was finished in red and featured plated tailgate chains with locking hooks. This truck was one of Tonka's most popular vehicles to replicate.

The No. 750-5 Carnation Milk Truck was also introduced in 1955. Although the truck used the same tooling as the 1954 Parcel Delivery Van, the color and decals were different. The only other difference between the new Carnation truck and the original 1954 model was that the step for the new side door was made with embossed aluminum rather than painted steel. There are actually two versions of the Carnation truck, thanks to a pattern developed by Tonka that seemed to underline many of the company's products.

Wenkstern (in boxcar) and Batdorf in the shipping area. 1955.
Lloyd L. Laumann collection

1955 Carnation Milk Truck.

Lee Klancher

On the first version of the 750-5 Carnation Milk Truck, of which only a few thousand were built, there is an International Trademark decal in the center of the grille. The decal is oval-shaped and features three blue diamonds with the word "International." International script lettering also appears directly above the front wheel well of the truck. The only problem with this early version is that Tonka didn't secure a licensing agreement with International to use their trademark logo, so all references to International were eliminated. This situation also happened with Tonka's AAA tow truck, and very few were built with the actual AAA design. It was quickly pointed out that this was a trademark infringement, and the decal was changed to "AA" with the big "A" removed from the center of the decal. Collectors of Tonkas from the mid-1950s should keep their eyes open for anomalies such as these. Tonka obtained design and logo trademark approval prior to use beginning in the late 1950s. Tonka began to publicly acknowledge license agreements beginning with the 1976 catalog.

Although Crounse, Tesch, and Baker had originally formed a company known as Mound Metalcraft, it was now time to face reality. The name "Tonka" had become a household word. Practically everyone in the United States knew that Tonka built toy trucks. The Mound Metalcraft name remained in the distant background, but on November 22, 1955, the company's name was changed from Mound Metalcraft Incorporated to Tonka Toys Incorporated. There was no change in ownership or management. The move was made to capitalize on Tonka's nationally distributed line of scale model trucks and to establish better product-manufacturer identification among consumers and the toy trade in general. Production under the Tonka Toys name began in 1955 and used the old logo, but that changed in 1956, as all toys built after that would carry a redesigned Tonka logo.

Tonka logo from 1956 to 1961.
Lee Klancher

The 1955 Aerial Ladder. The identity of the "fire chief" in the photo is unknown. *Lloyd L. Laumann collection*

Lucy Thurk, photographed in 1966, was one of the first female supervisors at Tonka. *Lloyd L. Laumann collection*

For 1956, Tonka employed 403 people and experienced a 35 percent sales increase for the year. Tonka's business was growing, but this was once again a tribute to the motivation of the people who worked there.

The progressive style of Tonka's business culture would become evident in later years in many different ways. In a move that was certainly on the cutting edge of the American business, Tonka appointed several women to key operational management positions. Gwen Cressy, who had started with Tonka on September 25, 1947, was named supervisor of the day-shift final assembly department, and Lucy Thurk, who started with Tonka on July 24, 1952, became the night-shift supervisor of the final assembly department. These positions were not taken lightly, as both of these women were the last line of defense in the quality-check process. "When they offered me the job, I took it right away," Cressy said in a 2004 interview. As a woman in charge of one of Tonka's most critical departments, Cressy readily admits that she was on new ground in American business.

The No. 0950-6 Suburban Pumper was
a great toy to play with (or annoy your
brother) on a hot summer day in 1956.
Lloyd L. Laumann collection

Tonka received an award for a toy that was designed by Charles M. Groschen and introduced in 1956. The Toy Guidance Council voted Tonka's Suburban Pumper the "Outstanding Example of American Toy Production" for 1956. The Pumper also received recognition from Science and Mechanics magazine as one of the top 10 mechanical toys. The Pumper Fire Truck's realistic features reflect the talents of Groschen and Tonka's product development team, who used a truck operated by the Mound Fire Department as inspiration for the fire truck. The real fire truck was built by the General Fire and Safety Equipment Company of North Branch, Minnesota, and Groschen's design of the truck was a big hit. The retail price on the Pumper was $8.98. It featured functional cabinet doors and hoses, which attached to the Pumper, and an accompanying fire hydrant. The hydrant could be hooked up to a garden hose, and the truck sprayed water through its hose. Finished in red with excellent decals, the Pumper was a sharp-looking toy that offered many hours of fun.

As if moving into the new facility was not enough for 1955, construction for a new 50,000-square-foot addition began in the fall of 1956. It was completed and up and running for the 1957 product line. A number of management promotions occurred in 1957. On January 31, Lynn Baker announced the promotion of Gordon Batdorf to executive vice president. Russell Wenkstern was promoted to vice president of manufacturing, and T. G. "Ted" Shaefer stepped up to vice president of sales. Many former employees who were familiar with Tonka's top management have noted that there existed a rivalry between Batdorf and Wenkstern that was never officially resolved. Each man had a vision of how Tonka should grow, and between them was Lynn Baker, who had reduced his duties with Tonka to the point that he spent six months in Minnesota and the other half of the year in Florida. There was also tension between Baker and Batdorf. Baker relinquished the presidency in 1961 and continued to be chairman of the board on the condition that Batdorf wouldn't assume the presidency. Tonka's board of directors was expanded with the addition of Florence E. Baker. Officially, Mrs. Baker knew little of the toy industry, and many speculated that the addition of Baker's wife to the board was a move to solidify Baker's name and presence on the board. Tonka's board of directors expanded again in 1958 with the addition of Clarence O. Holten, a Minneapolis attorney. The board members thought Holten would serve Tonka well as a corporate legal counsel and corporate secretary.

Employment reached 500 people during the summer of 1957. The workers were now spread out over 83,200 square feet of manufacturing space, and Tonka offered the largest selection of models in its history. A total of 38 different toys were being produced at the Mound plant, and 14 of those were new for 1957. The overall look of Tonka's products reached unprecedented quality, as the new electrostatic painting process was in full use. A careful inspection of Tonka's post-1957 products reveals that paint finishes were smooth and glossy with very few inconsistencies.

The year 1958 was a year of big changes at Tonka Toys. A major recession in the U.S. economy resulted in a noticeable decline in sales. As the economy sputtered, many of Tonka's retail customers were hedging on the delivery of finished products for fear they wouldn't be able to sell them. Tonka produced toys at the regular rate, but warehouses filled up as orders were put on hold. Tonka purchased an old creamery in Loretto, Minnesota, in 1954, and this building was used as a light-assembly building and storage facility for finished products. Tonka's leaders firmly believed that all of the toys would sell for the Christmas sea-

1957 No. 20 Hydraulic Dump.
Lee Klancher

son, so production was not scaled back. Retailers wanted to wait for delivery until just before Christmas, so the toys piled up. Toys were stored in barns, vacant houses, garages, and even a vacant movie theater in Mound. Gordon Batdorf remembers the chaos of 1958. "We were stuffing toys in any place we could find—incomplete homes, barns, et cetera—because none of the retailers wanted to take delivery early in 1958." In the end, Tonka's management had read the crystal ball correctly, and all storage facilities were empty by Christmas.

Tonka was on the cutting edge of manufacturing when it introduced its first progressive die, which formed pickup fenders. This type of tooling streamlined manufacturing, increased output, and decreased safety hazards. The die was complex and consisted of several operations that occurred with each cycle of the press, such as blank, emboss, pierce, form, trim, and final form. The coiled steel fed into the die progressed to the next station in the die with

Profile
Gerald Babb

Gerald Babb began work at Tonka Toys in 1959, and he remembers it like it was yesterday. His mother was Tonka employee number 19, and she ran a press there for most of her life. "I literally grew up with Tonka, so it was only natural that I wound up working there." As a materials handler, Babb was responsible for moving barrels of parts around so the toys could be assembled. "I would start in the morning, and the first thing to do was load about 30 barrels of parts that had been manufactured on the overnight shift onto a truck that took them to the assembly plant on Shoreline Boulevard," he said. Babb reckons that he rode the elevator between the three floors of the old school building several thousand times. He worked in materials for several years and then moved into the paint line. "We used the electrostatic method, which improved our paint quality tremendously," he said.

Babb was part of a unique period in Tonka's history when he was assigned to the department that manufactured tires. For a brief time, Tonka manufactured their own rubber tires after they were outsourced from an outside vendor. "We bought all of the equipment, trained all the people, and ran it for one year. Then, Tonka decided to go into plastic injection molding," Babb said. He also holds the distinctive honor of being the youngest supervisor Tonka ever had. He attained the position at the age of 22, and he was a supervisor in the plastic injection department until he left the company in 1982.

According to Babb, "Tonka was a great place to work, and I have many fond memories of working there." He remembers one day when torrential rains threatened the building due to a blocked drainage culvert. Babb volunteered to jump into a hole filled with water to clear the drain, and when he emerged from the hole, he was greeted by Russ Wenkstern who said, "You did a good job." Babb enjoyed his years at Tonka, and he still sees many of the people he used to work with. "Tonka was a good place to work, and they allowed their employees to grow with the company."

each hit. After the successful introduction of the progressive pickup fender die, Tonka followed with numerous progressive dies. Eventually Tonka purchased a progressive truck cab die that provided a complete cab wrap in one press. Previous to the progressive die method, employees would hold a piece of flat metal under the press until the die made its hit, then an employee would transfer the piece to another press where the next die hit was made. This was a slow, hazardous, labor-intensive process. Utilizing the progressive dies, Tonka manufactured over 10,000 trucks per day.

A major announcement was delivered at the 1958 New York Toy Fair with the introduction of a new-styled cab for Tonka trucks. The cab, roof, grille, and headlights were all

1957 No. 44 3 in 1 Hi-Way Service Truck with Plow and Blade.
Lee Klancher

1959 Dump Truck.
Dennis David

changed. A comparison between the new style for 1958 and the Ford's trucks from the same year have many similarities. Tonka employees began referring to the new style as the "box" or rectangular truck, due in part to the squared-off hood and flush fenders. The new style marked the first time a Tonka truck had a clear plastic windshield. The truck still retained the hubcaps with round holes, but this was their last year. A new hubcap with triangular holes made its debut in 1959.

Tonka ventured to a new untapped frontier in 1958. Knowing that Americans loved their leisure time, Tonka introduced the No. 05 Sportsman. The Sportsman was nothing more than Tonka's No. 02 pickup truck with a steel sportsman top. It was painted in dark blue and featured the Tonka logo on each door. This truck inspired many recreational vehicles that generated healthy profits for Tonka in later years. Jeeps, Jeepsters, boats, campers, and trailers of all kinds became a large portion of Tonka's production lines.

Tonka led the toy truck manufacturing industry in the late 1950s. The Mound, Minnesota, plant turned out toys by the thousands, and children everywhere loved them. The year 1958 was a banner year for Tonka, and with the 1960s just around the corner, Tonka was poised to become the undisputed king of toy truck builders.

Fast Fact

THE PROGRESSIVE DIE-STAMPING SYSTEM

Tonka's research and development leader Charles Groschen recalled in a 2004 interview how the numbers worked when they calculated the productivity improvement with the new progressive die. "Before the progressive die, it took seven presses, seven dies, and seven workers to make 5,000 pairs of pickup truck fenders in eight hours." Groschen was concerned about the number of parts produced per shift, but his primary concern was safety. "With the standard press-type system, you have to place your hands in the machine and even with double hand trips, accidents can happen." Groschen recalled that Tonka was 35 percent below the national average for safety, and he knew a progressive die-stamping line would enhance safety because it meant fewer hands in dangerous areas. "At the time, it required an investment of around $35,000, but I assured management that it would pay for itself." Groschen's forecast called for the line to pay for itself within 18 months, but the line actually paid for itself within the first year. "After we installed the line, we were able to produce 40,000 pairs of fenders in one eight-hour shift using just one person." This actually created new problems because fenders for Tonka's pickup trucks were being produced ahead of production of the trucks themselves. "The fenders had to be separated between left and right, then stored in bags to protect them from the elements."

The progressive die method had proven itself at Tonka, and eventually all of the toy lines were turned over to the new method. "We actually ended up being 35 percent better than the national average in safety due to the new system, and that put a big smile on my face," Groschen said.

Manufacturing has come a long way since the 1960s, and safety has been a paramount issue with every major company since the beginning. Groschen's efforts made for a safer workplace, and he's just another example of the people at Tonka who made a difference.

Chapter 6

1959–1961

Many historians have noted that the 1960s was a decade of turbulence in America. With the passing of the 1950s, controversy seemed to be everywhere as the nation struggled for direction in everything from politics to foreign relations. In the midst of all of this controversy was the diversion of toys. If the 1950s were a great time to be a child, the 1960s were a very trying time to be a parent. As America polarized in its viewpoints on major issues, parents attempted to shield their growing children from the storms of controversy. This may have involved trips to the local amusement park or a family vacation in the station wagon. Whether at home or in the car, the most prominent diversionary tactics were toys.

As Tonka entered the 1960s, it did so with many new products to offer. It was a very ambitious year for a company that had come from a fledgling idea of three very different men to a multimillion dollar corporation in 14 years. Tonka Toys now employed 500 people and was considered by many to be the number one manufacturer of metal toy trucks. During peak production, Tonka's output was 10,000 toys per day. As the nation prepared to enter the new decade, Tonka Toys made several major changes to its toys that gave them a fresh look. All of these changes took place on the 1959 models to prepare for the new decade.

1961 Allied Van.
Lee Klancher

No. 40 Car Carrier, No. 42 Hydraulic
Land Rover, and No. 41 Boat Transport
from 1959.

Lloyd L. Laumann collection

A total of 43 models comprised Tonka's offerings for 1959; 16 were completely new designs, 24 had various upgrades and changes, and only 3 were carried over with no changes at all. Tonka added plastic accessories to some of their toys in the late 1950s, and all of this work was contracted out. This changed on January 1, 1959, when Tonka formed a wholly owned subsidiary called Empire Plastic. This company provided Tonka with the plastic accessories needed for its toy line, and it also did some contract work for other companies in the Mound area. This wasn't Tonka's first holding of a separate company, as they later acquired Gresen Manufacturing.

Empire Plastic was located in the old creamery building in Loretto, Minnesota, that Tonka had used for manufacturing and storage for several years. A total of 5,000 square feet were added, and the building housed injection-molding machines for plastic. By manufacturing their own plastic parts, Tonka was able to save money and ensure the quality, scheduling, and inventory of parts.

Tonka trucks received a new hubcap for 1959 that featured triangular pierced holes. A solid disc-style wheel cover that featured five simulated lug nuts was also used, but the triangular hole hubcap founds its way onto the majority of 1959 Tonka trucks and construction

A photo from a sales meeting that was held in Florida in 1960.
Lloyd L. Laumann collection

TONKA TOY ACCESSORIES

Tonka Toys INC.
MOUND, MINNESOTA

1960

The Finest Quality at the Lowest Price in Metal Toys

MOUND, MINNESOTA

NO. AC316 CORRAL AND FOUR FARM ANIMALS Polystyrene animals romp inside natural wood, six-sided corral. Height just right for loading chute just right for No. 04 Farm Stake and No. AC312 Stake Trailer. Fence sections are 9½" long. Assembled corral 19" across $2.98

AC310 BOX TRAILER Adds new to present toys. Attaches to No. 02 and No. 28 Pick-Ups, No. 04 and 35 Farm Stakes, No. 05 Sportsman, No. 22 Deluxe Sportsman, No. 110 Fisherman and No. 130 Deluxe Fisherman. A sturdy 8½" x 3¾" x 5¼" trailer, it's good for years of hauling service $1.98

NO. AC312 STAKE TRAILER Just the thing to shuttle livestock and other precious playtime cargoes. End panel removable. Attaches to same trucks as Box Trailer above, though slightly bigger (8½" x 4¼" x 5") $1.98

NO. AC314 HORSE TRAILER AND TWO HORSES Provides extra fun for any play hour. Proud and poised black beauties are made of polystyrene and durable as their steel trailer. 8½" x 4¼" x 5¼" trailer attaches to same trucks as Box Trailer above $2.98

NO. AC330 THE FALCON This car is an exact duplicate of the real Falcon. Youngster will enjoy having the newest car in the block. Comes in 3 colors . . . . . . each $ .98

NO. AC308 SCALE MODEL CARS A child never has too many cars. These low-priced models are made of polyethylene and will stand up under a lot of hard mileage. No. 40 Car Carrier will transport 5 of them. Available in 3 colors . . . . . . each $ .98

NO. AC320 HI-WAY SIGN SET 6 signs and 2 road barriers put more realism into road building projects, stimulates educational interest in highway safety and rules of the road. Signs are 4½" high, barriers 4½" x 6" $2.98

NO. AC319 SNOW PLOW AND BRACKET Also made to fit No. 06 and No. 20 Dump Trucks. Constructed of real steel, 9" blade is perfect replica of real snow plow. Plenty of extra fun for imaginative child $1.98

NO. AC318 SCRAPER BLADE AND BRACKET Made for easy installation on No. 06 and No. 20 Dump Trucks. The addition of 7" steel scraper blade will give truck all the appeal of a new toy . . . . . . $1.4(

NO. AC325 ASSORT(...) MALS Make welcome (...) corral stock. Can b(...) Box, Stake, or Hors(...) in No. 02 and No. (...) No. 04 and No. 35 (...) Realistic farm ani(...) durable polystyre(...)

If you are unable to find the Tonka Toy Accessory yo(...)
order blank.

I wish to purchase Model No. _____ Check o(...)

Name _____

Address _____ Zone _____

City _____

Mail to: TONKA TOYS, I(...)

All items (...)

MARINE ACC(...)

NO. AC345 DELUXE BOAT Sporty boat for young fisherman. Equipped with windshield, seats, deck, and scale-model outboard motor that is detachable. Made of unbreakable polyethylene. 9" long $1.29

NO. AC350 DELUXE BOAT AND TRAILER Makes a wonderful tow-around toy. Trailer made of enameled steel and mounted on white sidewall tires. Elastic strap secures boat. Easy to launch. Couples to No. 02 and No. 28 Pick-Ups, No. 04 and No. 35 Farm Stakes, No. 05 Sportsman, No. 22 Deluxe Sportsman, No. 110 Fisherman and No. 130 Deluxe Fisherman $1.98

NO. AC37(...) head for th(...) winch for (...) mounted or (...) can be cou(...) No. 35 Farm(...) man, No. 11(...)

ACCESSORY PACKA(...)

Tonka Toys INC.
MOUND, MINNESOTA

NO. AC300 TONKA ACCESSORY SET The whole splendid array of Tonka Toy mobile accessories all in one exciting package. Will make a youngster literally jump for joy. Set includes AC350 Deluxe Boat and Trailer, AC370 Tonka Clipper and Trailer, AC310 Box Trailer, AC312 Stake Trailer, and AC314 Horse Trailer and Two Horses $11.95

designed for child development

1960 accessories flyer.
Lloyd L. Laumann collection

toys. The tires were also changed for 1959 when they received a large cutout that accommodated a white sidewall insert. The LaValle Rubber Company supplied the tire and rubber insert. Tonka's solid black tire was still produced by the Nye Rubber Company. Tonka also used a new style of tire on its No. 42 Hydraulic Land Rover, which was a special swamp tire that didn't use the standard Tonka hubcap. This was an unusual-looking tire that required a derby-shaped nut that served as a hubcap.

For 1960, Tonka's offerings were unequalled in the toy industry. Twenty-nine individual toys were offered, as well as nine sets and 15 different accessories. Sales increased by 24 percent from the previous year, and net profits stood at $159,323. Two additions were made to the plant for 1960 with a 24,000-square-foot addition to the main building and the acquisition of Mound Motors, which was converted into a tool room. Land on the east and west ends of the plant was also purchased with an eye on future expansion. The various phases of Tonka's expansion can be seen on a drive along Shoreline Drive in present-day Mound. The quarter-mile-long building displays the different sections that were added on over the years. Each addition speaks of a different era in Tonka's expansion and subsequent domination of the toy truck industry.

Tonka logos
1956-1961

Tonka's business structure changed drastically on July 5, 1960, when common stock was offered to the public through the American Stock Exchange. Gordon Batdorf remembers the day that Tonka went public. "We thought it would initially be offered at $6 per share, but the company handling it for us had upped it to $12. By the time the day was over, Tonka's stock trading under the name TKA had closed at $18 per share." By December 1961, Tonka's stock was trading at $31 per share. The active and upward climb of Tonka's stock price attracted the attention of financial backers and investors throughout the nation.

A new offering in 1960 was the No. 100 Bulldozer. The 1960 Bulldozer is unique for several reasons. The steel roller wheels for the tracks were plated, and a No. 100 decal was placed on the hood. The dozer was painted orange, but all of this changed in 1961. Tonka presented a new dozer chassis that enclosed the new black plastic roller wheels. The decals used in 1960 were reused for the 1961 dozer. Tonka's 1960 No. 01 Service Truck was modified and introduced as the No. 105 Rescue Squad Truck. The No. 105 was painted a glossy white and featured a ladder

1959 No. 06 Dump Truck.
Lee Klancher

and a polyethylene boat strapped to the top. The truck also featured an emergency light on the roof, and a die-cast metal siren was mounted to the driver's side front fender, similar to the fire truck of the same year. A "Civil Defense" decal appears on each side-door panel, and a bold "Rescue Squad" decal with a red cross between the two words appears on each side of the box. In 1960, the Rescue Squad Truck was sold with the Fire Department set. In 1961 the Rescue Squad Truck was sold alone and was never to be seen again after that year. They remain a rarity in the Tonka line.

Tonka continued to expand its leisure vehicles as the concept of hitting the road for the great American vacation took hold. For 1960, the No. 110 Fisherman Pickup Truck was Tonka's first edition of a styleside design. The smooth flow of the rear fender section allowed

An Aerial Ladder from the early 1960s.
Dennis David

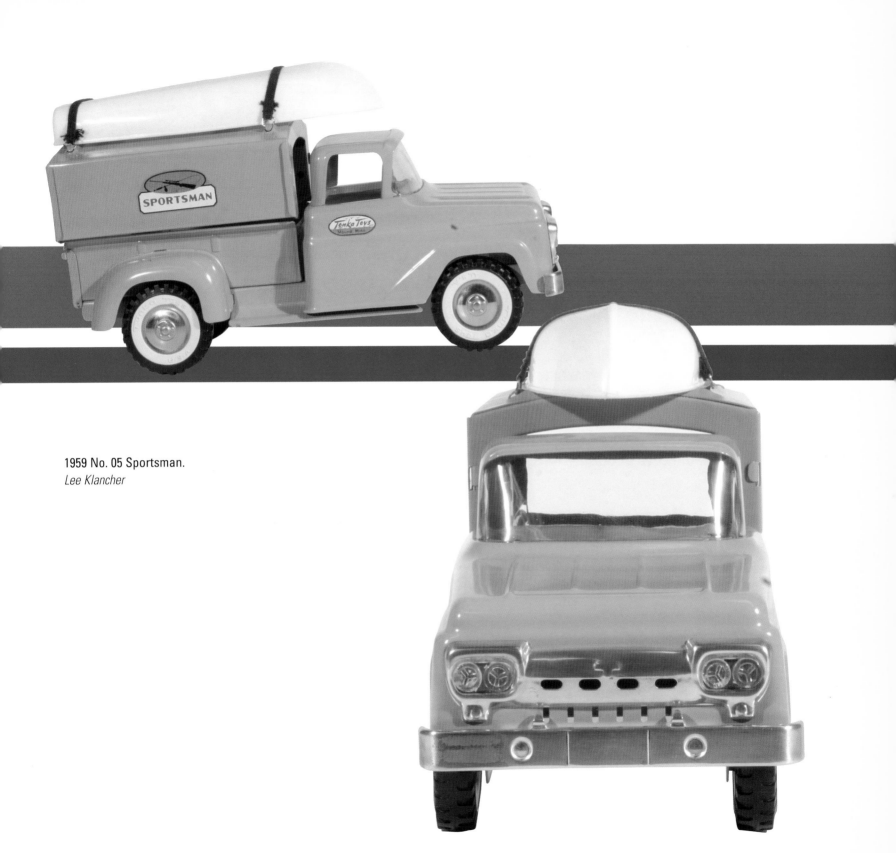

1959 No. 05 Sportsman.
Lee Klancher

Profile
Gwen Cressy

Gwen Cressy (right) and Lucy Thurk (left) both had unique experiences in their years with Tonka. During the 1960s, when the concept of women in management positions was still in its infancy in the American business world, both were final assembly supervisors in charge of over 300 people each. Thurk passed away in 1982, but Cressy is still enjoying her retirement and remembers her 26 years with Tonka. Although she started as an assembler in the original schoolhouse in 1947, she worked her way up, and by the 1960s she held the title of day final assembly supervisor at the new plant. "When they offered me the job, I took it right away," she said. At the height of her employment with Tonka, she was in charge of the department that did the final assembly work for many of Tonka's toys. "I look back on those times as the best years of my life," said Cressy, who still keeps in touch with many former Tonka employees. As one of the original employees of Mound Metalcraft, she knew the three founders of Tonka very well. "I always wondered how the three of them got together to form a company because they were all so different," Cressy said. "Lynn Baker was a pretty straight-forward person who sometimes kept his distance from the factory floor, while Crounse and Tesch were more approachable," she said. Her impression of Crounse and Tesch was that they always had their feet firmly planted on the ground and mingled with the employees, but Baker was a little more reserved. Cressy sadly recalls when Tonka left Mound. "So many people had jobs there, and Tonka was a part of Mound's identity."

When Gwen sees a Tonka toy on the shelf at a local toy store, it brings back the many fond memories she has of working at Tonka "I recently bought a Tonka Mighty Dump Truck as a gift for my great-grandson, and he loved it!" She said about her years at Tonka, "It was really a great place to work and they treated us so well."

Cressy occasionally passes the Mound plant that holds so many memories for her. "Sometimes I have to look away, but most times I just glance at it and smile." As a supervisor at a major manufacturing plant in the 1960s, Cressy helped blaze a path that many women have chosen to follow. "They were a great company to work for. Tonka believed in me, and they gave me a chance to prove myself." One needs only to look at one of Tonka's original toys from the early years to prove that Cressy, Thurk, and their coworkers took their work seriously.

1960 Cement Mixer.
Dennis David

the truck to carry a bigger topper on its rear bed. The concept of the styleside pickup was taken directly from Detroit, as many of the nation's car companies also featured a styleside pickup. The "Tonka Toys" name was embossed on the truck's tailgate, but this was the first and only year for this feature. After 1960, only the word "Tonka" was embossed on the tailgate. Although the Fisherman Pickup Truck used the new styleside design, the rest of Tonka's pickup trucks continued to use a round rear fender.

Tonka's No. 120 Cement Mixer was also new for 1960. The unique feature of the mixer was that the drum turned as the truck was pushed across the floor. This was accomplished by a set of gears with a drive shaft that turned from the front axle. The mixer drum was constructed from Implex plastic, a material tough enough to stand the rigors of outdoor play. The truck was finished in brilliant red and was impressive. The mixer was refined several times over the years, and Tonka marketed a mixer in various product lines through 1991.

Tonka made so many improvements to the Sanitary Truck in 1960 that a new stock number

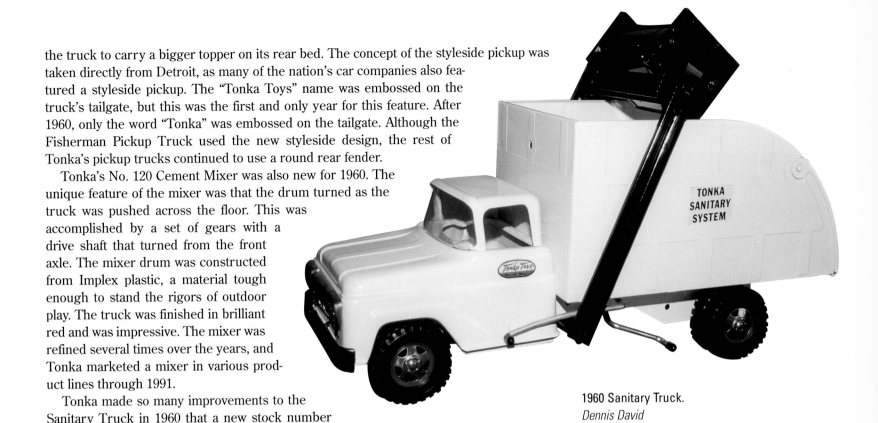

1960 Sanitary Truck.
Dennis David

Profile
Joyce Flusemann

Joyce Flusemann assembled many of Tonka's products in her 24 years with the company, but the toy she remembers most is the Mighty Dump Truck. As a final assembler on the Mighty line, she was assigned to assembly of the wheels and axles. "I couldn't even begin to tell you how many of those trucks I put together over the years," she said. Given that Tonka built several million Mighty Dumps, one would reason that she would have assembled at least a few hundred thousand. "Some days I'd do the axles, and other days I'd put them in boxes, but there sure were a lot of them," she said.

Tonka's assembly lines rivaled that of America's auto industry, and the coordination involved in keeping everything running was an incredible feat in itself. "We had a lead person who was responsible for keeping things going, but sometimes the trucks would come down the line too fast and we'd stack them up until we could get to them," she said. Flusemann's line was one of several assembly lines at Tonka, and she worked on the Mini line as well.

Flusemann stayed with Tonka until production moved in 1983. "It really hurt when they moved because I left a lot of friends behind," she said. Although she is now retired, she still sees many of her friends from Tonka. Flusemann is a typical Tonka employee, which many considered the company's greatest strength. "I enjoyed my years there, and I made friends for life."

was issued. The new No. 140 Sanitary Truck featured the 1960 cab design, and a new box was designed specifically for this model. The Sanitary Truck came with one hopper, and the forks mounted at the midpoint of the truck's chassis lifted the hopper and dumped it into the back of the truck. For 1961, the black-and-white Sanitary Truck used Tonka's new whitewall tire, but this truck is extremely difficult to locate because they were discontinued after a lawsuit. The focal point of the suit was the hydraulic cylinder, and Tonka dropped the truck from its lineup. It reappeared in 1967 without the hydraulic cylinder.

Tonka introduced the No. 101 Golf Cart Tractor in 1960, and in recent years, it has proven to be a very difficult item to find due to the limited number that were built. Tonka built only 20,000 of these tractor-type vehicles. The Golf Cart Tractor had a small dump body on the rear that featured dual rear wheels, a small seat, and an exposed plastic engine. The Golf Cart was also sold in 1961 in the No. B-202 Country Club Service Set. This set featured Tonka's No. 100 Bulldozer, No. 101 Golf Club Tractor, a yellow tilt-bed trailer borrowed from the No. 134 Grading Service set, and a seafoam green pickup truck based on the No. 22 Sportsman. Finding a Tonka Golf Cart in any condition is a rarity and makes a wonderful addition to anyone's collection.

With a firm grasp on the lead in toy vehicle manufacturing, Tonka was ready to branch out even more. The product line was diverse, and there was a truck for every purpose. Tonka was ready to enter a different market that did not involve a totally different type of vehicle, but a new venue that involved size.

1961 No. 101 Golf Club Tractor.
Dennis David

Fast Fact

PRODUCT TESTING

Many Tonka collectors have often noticed that no matter how old a Tonka is, they usually have most of their pieces still attached. This is due to Tonka's rigorous testing procedures to ensure that all new product designs met the highest standards of durability. Product testing has always been a major concern with any manufacturer, but the safety and durability of any product is no more important than in the toy industry. Tonka's product-testing program at its Mound facility was a process that tested the limits of each toy beyond what would be considered normal wear and tear. The testing process itself ensured that only the best designs wore the Tonka logo.

First, the toy underwent abuse testing. In this phase, the toys were rolled off of tables, dropped, and thrown into walls to make sure no small parts fell off. This test revealed any sharp edges exposed from missing pieces. Next came the drop test. In this phase, the toy was dropped from various heights to make sure it wouldn't crack or break. This test was repeated four times to be sure of the results.

One of the most troublesome components of a toy vehicle can be the wheels. Tonka's wheel pull test used 10 to 20 pounds of pressure to see if the wheels stayed put. The amount of pressure used in the test was determined by the size of the wheel and how it was attached. The next test involved a visual inspection of the toy for sharp edges, sharp points, and the size of small parts. This phase ensured that no child would be injured due to sharp edges and also exposed any choking hazards.

If the toy survived this far, it went to the bending test. This phase tested the durability for the wires and rods that were used on many Tonka Toys. These parts would be bent back and forth to a 120-degree angle to test their strength. Finally, there was the tumble test. For this phase, the toy was tumbled down a flight of six steps in various positions to determine the strength of its construction and parts attachment. This test was repeated eight times and is why many American households have nicks and scratches in their woodwork because Tonka's toys stayed in one piece.

At the end of the Tonka's testing phase, the toy had to meet standards set by the federal government relating to paint coatings, flammable materials, toxic substances, and electrical and thermal energy. As Tonka became a worldwide company, the standards of other countries also had to be met, but most were not as stringent as the United States.

Tonka's testing program was one of the finest programs of its kind. While the testing program certainly accounts for the number of Tonka Toys found in basements and attics with all of their parts intact, it also accounts for a margin of safety that made sure children playing with Tonka's toys were not harmed in any way.

Chapter 7
1961–1964

Tonka continued to expand its domination of the U.S. toy truck market in the early 1960s, and its line of toy trucks sold at an impressive rate. The progressive dies had increased productivity, and the company was capable of turning out more toys than ever.

Phenomenal growth was the key concept for the 1960s, and profits for 1961 alone were $398,444, which was an incredible 150 percent increase over the previous year. In December 1961, Tonka's stock on the New York Stock Exchange traded at $31 per share. The year 1961 also marked a changing of the guard at Tonka as Lynn Baker's health problems forced him to remove himself from day-to-day operations. Russell Wenkstern was appointed president, and Gordon Batdorf was made executive vice president. Together, these two men and Charlie Groschen guided Tonka through several expansions at the Mound plant and introduced many new products during the 1960s. Wenkstern essentially had the official responsibility of running the company, and Baker still maintained his presence as chairman of Tonka's board of directors. Given the success of Tonka's products in the 1960s, the formula that Wenkstern, Batdorf, and Groschen used was well received, profits were up, and employee morale was positive.

1964 No. 425 Jeep Pumper.
Dennis David

With Wenkstern and Batdorf at the helm, along with significant input from Groschen and Tonka representatives, product design continued to be a major focus. The successful look of 1960 was carried over with only minor modifications. A new addition to the 1961 line was the No. 116 Dump Truck and Sand Loader. This nifty toy allowed a youngster to load the dump truck with sand by turning the crank on the loader, which moved a conveyor belt that carried the sand. The conveyor belt was actually a bulldozer tread borrowed from Tonka's Giant Dozer. Realistic action contributed to the success of this toy, which was manufactured until 1970.

The No. 117 Boat Service Truck was also introduced in 1961. It is an extremely rare toy because it was built for only one year. The truck had a beautiful sea-foam-green-and-white two-tone body and hauled a unique trailer that held three boats. The three boats were made of molded plastic with different colored parts. The boat on top featured a deck with a clear plastic windshield. Sales of the Boat Service Truck were disappointing, and it was considered a failure. This truck-and-trailer model is very rare and almost impossible to find today. Tonka's plastic boats were also hauled on the No. 41 Boat Transport. This truck hauled four of Tonka's plastic boats, which were delivered by sliding the boats off the back. Tonka discovered the unique appeal of toy boats, as the No. 136 Houseboat was also introduced for 1961. This toy boat measured 13 inches long and was molded in bright red-and-white plastic parts.

In mid-1961, Tonka's management team began to explore the idea of diversification. Knowing that a day might come when Tonka would need to offer more than just toys, a new logo was designed to simplify the Tonka name. This new logo, which appeared on all company stationery in July 1961, was used on all Tonka products beginning in February 1962. A significant milestone was reached in 1962 when sales and production exceeded $10 million. The success of the 1962 product line, which consisted of 40 models, 34 individual toys, and six sets resulted in double the amount of orders on hand through June 1962 from the previous year.

Much of the success for 1962 can be attributed to an agreement forged between Tonka and the Willys/Jeep Company to manufacture a line of Jeep replicas. According to Tonka authority Lloyd Lauman, the logic used at the time was simple. "We were able to sell the Jeep line for under three dollars, and this brought in a whole new market. Any toy that sold for less than three dollars could easily be marketed all year-round as birthday presents, coming-home gifts, and as an impulse purchase. Toys that sold in excess of five dollars generally were limited to Christmas-season sales." The new No. 200 Jeep Dispatcher was the start of a product line that produced huge profits for Tonka. The Jeep was also used in several configurations throughout the years. For 1962, this toy alone claimed the top sales position at Tonka.

Logo from 1962 to 1969.

Lloyd L. Laumann collection

Opposite: A page out of the June 1962 *Upper Midwest Investor*.

Lloyd L. Laumann collection

Gordon Batdorf shows Tonka Toys to visitors at Investor's Forum in Minneapolis.

with hooks dip the gray bodies into a solution that cleans off the oil (lubricant from the presses) and then into a vat of primer paint. From there, a second coat is applied uniformly by an electro-static device which flings charged particles of paint at the circulating metal bodies.

Long rows of drying ovens are next on the route, and after that the bodies move into final assembly, where more quick hands put on tires, headlights, grilles, windshields and decals. Each completed toy is inspected before packaging. Finally, conveyor belts move boxed toys to the huge warehouse, out of which a half million dollars worth of inventory is loaded into trucks and freightcars every ten working days.

The quick hands mentioned above belong to over 700 employees. mostly women from Mound and neighboring communities who have worked for Tonka for years and have participated in its growth. Ordinarily, seasonal layoffs mean a perennial problem of securing labor and preventing high training costs, but not so at Tonka. The majority of the women work to augment family income and consider their jobs well worth coming back to year after year.

Labor relations have always been outstanding. A rare spirit of camaraderie exists at Tonka, where management and workers greet each other by first names (Wenkstern and Batdorf both live in Mound, a small community, and know virtually all employees by name). Goals, policies and problems are discussed plantwide; and

nies, what it will cost to produce a new toy.

The surrey jeep posed a problem because a fast and economical method of attaching the fringe had to be devised if the company was to sell the toy at a competitive price. In time, Groschen and his associates perfected an assembly machine which glued and attached a fringe to a top in seconds, permitting the surrey jeep to go on the market at $3.50.

In spite of increasing costs and wage rates, Tonka's price structure is remarkably stable. Suggested retail prices range from $2 to $13 per individual toy and $10 to $19 per combination set. (For example, the road builder set consists of a grader, dump truck, sand loader, bulldozer and trailer; it sells for $15).

Thanks to production line efficiency and automation, direct labor costs are only 13 per cent of sales. However, automation has never laid off a worker at Tonka. According to Wenkstern, "Our business has been expanding so rapidly there is always something new for displaced workers to do."

An example of Tonka's automation is seen in the double row of punch presses at the beginning of the production line. Clacking away at a fast rate, these mammoth machines turn rolls of 19-gauge steel

(the body on your car is 20-gauge) into elaborate parts. One press, with progressive dies, will cut, shape and mold in one operation a fender that formerly required seven separate steps.

To conserve capital for expansion, Tonka leases its presses, some with 150 tons capacity; it has 35 in operation and another 150-ton press on order.

The punched out parts are fed into the pre-assembly section on conveyor belts where quick hands join, weld or rivet them into body shells. Overhead conveyor lines

Assembly, inspection and packaging occupy many of Tonka's 685 employees.

No. 200 Jeep Dispatcher.
Dennis David

The new Jeep design marked a milestone for Tonka in 1962 and became the basis for a toy marketed to girls. The genesis of this toy began when Earle Colee, Tonka's western sales representative, took a vacation to Mexico in early 1961. While he was in Acapulco, he saw a Jeep Surrey that featured a fringe top used by the local hotel for transporting guests. Upon his return, Colee immediately contacted Tonka president Russ Wenkstern and convinced him that the Jeep should be part of the 1962 product line. Tonka's product development team, led by Charlie Groschen, went to work on it immediately, but there was one problem. The team had to come up with a fast and economical way to attach the fringe to the surrey's top without excessive labor costs. Groschen and his team spent many hours developing an assembly machine that glued the fringe to the top in seconds. The No. 350 Jeep Surrey received an enthusiastic response at the New York Toy Fair and sold 500,000 units during its first year. Tonka had finally captured the attention of girls everywhere, who just couldn't get enough of the pink Jeep with the fringe top. The pink surrey had done what the No. 300 Tonka Doll Bed could not, and the Tonka name was now solidified with girls, as well as boys. Many female Tonka employees used their pink surrey as a jewelry box.

Opposite: 1962 No. 350 Jeep Surrey on the cover of the 1962 catalog.
Lloyd L. Laumann collection

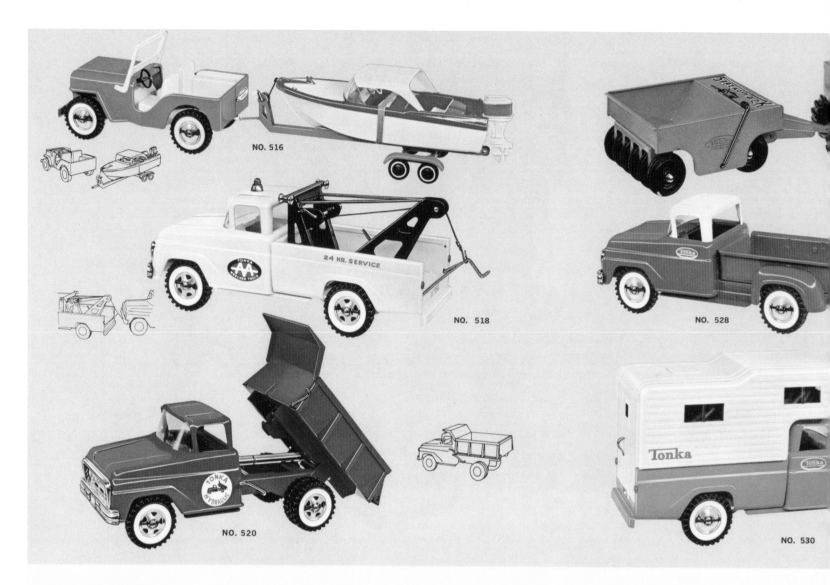

Tonka

MOUND, MINNESOTA

1962

NO. 516—'JEEP' RUNABOUT Sporty-looking combination no child can resist. Has steering wheel, front seats, real white sidewall tires, and custom chrome discs. Realistically designed boat, with windshield, canopy, and detachable motor, is mounted on tandem wheel trailer. Winch pulls boat on trailer. 24⅝″ long, 5⅜″ high, 5⅛″ wide. Packed 6 to a shipper, weight 19 lbs. **$5.00**

NO. 518—WRECKER Broken toys suddenly become fun to play with again. Newly restyled Wrecker can rescue stalled or overturned trucks. Heavy-duty winch is supported by reinforcing bars. Engage nylon cable hook to bumper bar and turn crank to raise disabled vehicle. Equipped with "flasher" light and white sidewall tires. 14¼″ long, 6″ high, 5½″ wide. Packed 6 to a shipper, weight 24 lbs. **$5.00**

NO. 520—HYDRAULIC DUMP A dump truck that actually unloads automatically. A touch on the release lever and the load is raised smoothly and hydraulically by safety-type cylinder. The 2-position tailgate permits straight dumping or spreading. Comes with white sidewall tires and dual rear wheels. 13½″ long, 6¼″ high, 6¼″ wide. Packed 6 to a shipper, weight 25 lbs. **$5.00**

NO. 524—DOZER PACKER Exactly like the equipment used to build real highways. Dozer moves on deep-grooved treads. Blade can be adjusted to 3 positions by lever. Easily detachable Packer equipped with 11 rubber tires. Lever on side opens bottom of unit to permit fine spr[...] units constructed of steel [...] durability. 18¼″ long, 4[...] wide. Packed 6 to a shi[...] 22 lbs. . . . .

NO. 528—PICK-UP AN[...] A three-piece toy that w[...] boy a farmer. All-steel Pi[...] hauls Stake Trailer with [...] styrene animal. Simple [...] gether. End stake panels [...] out for loading. Truck t[...] and closes. 20¾″ over-all[...]

1962 Tonka catalog.

Lloyd L. Laumann collection

Tonka marketed its first tractor in 1962. The hood, engine, and grille for the No. 250 Tractor were taken from the parts bin of the No. 101 Golf Club Tractor and were painted orange. Tonka changed the colors of this toy over the next two years in an attempt to generate consumer interest, but it never caught on. In 1973, another Tonka farm tractor appeared and gained some success in the product line. Tonka found another use for the golf club tractor tooling in the No. 420 Luggage Service vehicle. In an attempt to capitalize on the increasing popularity of air travel in the early 1960s, this wonderful toy displayed Tonka's commitment to providing children with toys that inspired the imagination. The Luggage Service vehicle was finished in light blue and came with an open-sided cart that carried five polystyrene suitcases. The side of the hood on this toy said "Tonka Airlines."

Since the very beginning, Tonka manufactured a variety of toy vehicles, but they were all roughly the same scale. This changed in 1963 with the introduction of the Mini-Tonka line. The new Mini featured the same quality and realistic features, but in a smaller and

high, 5¼" wide. Pack
weight 26 lbs.

NO. 530—CAMPE
are exciting words
extra large Camper
room for equipment.
swings out for eas
five windows whi
side truck features
wall tires with c
discs. 14" long, 8
Packed 6 to a shi

1963 Dump Truck.
Dennis David

NO. 616

NO. 618

NO. 620

ALLIED
VAN LINES, INC
WORLD'S LARGEST MOVE

NO. 73

Tonka

MOUND, MINNESOTA

1962

NO. 616—DUMP TRUCK & SAND LOADER Now loading a dump truck is just as much fun as unloading. Endless belt operates by crank on top of Sand Loader. Hopper raised and lowered by lever on side. Dump Truck fully workable. Movable tailgate permits straight dumping or spreading. 23¼" long, 8½" high, 6¼" wide. Packed 4 to a shipper, weight 25 lbs.   **$6.00**

NO. 618 — GIANT DOZER This machine is designed to stand up to years of use and abuse. Its sturdy, all-steel body and heavy-duty blade make it the most rugged Tonka Toy built. Moves on soundless treads, deep-grooved for traction. Lever controls height of blade which adjusts to 3 positions. 12½" long, 5¾" high, 8¼" wide. Packed 4 to a shipper, weight 18 lbs. **$6.00**

NO. 620—CEMENT MIXER An exact model that works with perfect realism. Fills through hopper on top. Mixer assembly, made of all-weather, extra-tough plastic material, is geared to turn as truck moves. At "construction site," mixer tilts by handle to pour "cement" down adjustable chute. Tandem dual rubber white sidewall tires. 15½" long, 8" high, 6⅝" wide. Packed 4 to a shipper, weight 22 lbs. **$6.00**

NO. 735—FARM STAKE TRAILER It's off to the an exciting day of racing. Trailer carries two jet bla polystyrene plastic. Ba connects trailer to Farm Removable rounded-edge Genuine rubber white side truck and trailer. 21¾" l 6" wide. Packed 4 to a shi 25 lbs.

1962 Tonka catalog.
Lloyd L. Laumann collection

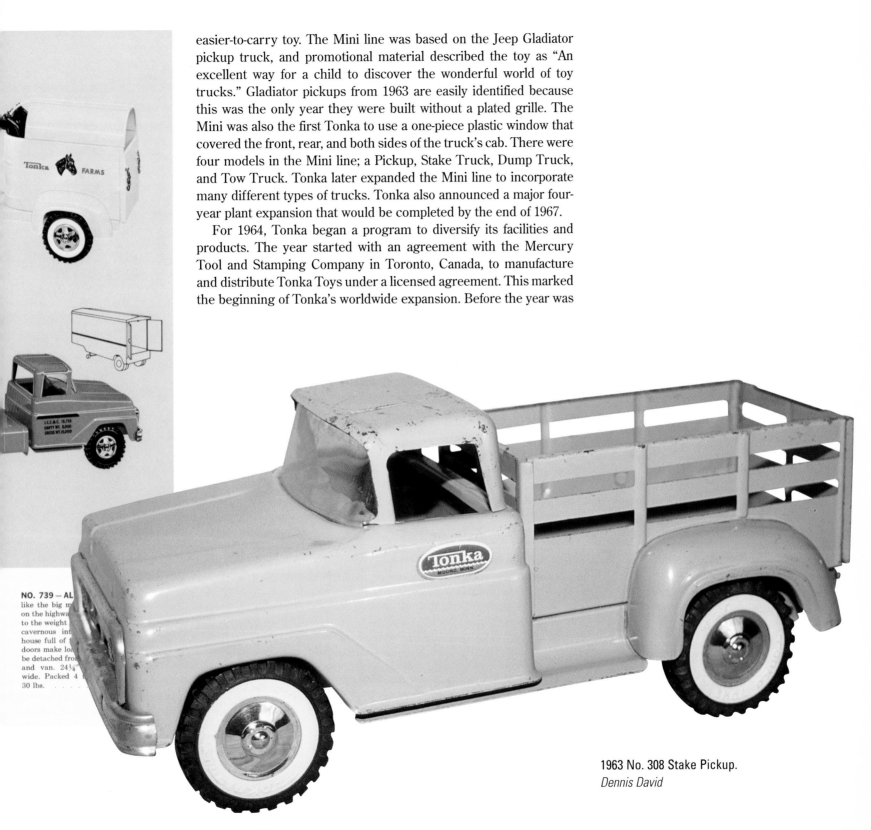

easier-to-carry toy. The Mini line was based on the Jeep Gladiator pickup truck, and promotional material described the toy as "An excellent way for a child to discover the wonderful world of toy trucks." Gladiator pickups from 1963 are easily identified because this was the only year they were built without a plated grille. The Mini was also the first Tonka to use a one-piece plastic window that covered the front, rear, and both sides of the truck's cab. There were four models in the Mini line; a Pickup, Stake Truck, Dump Truck, and Tow Truck. Tonka later expanded the Mini line to incorporate many different types of trucks. Tonka also announced a major four-year plant expansion that would be completed by the end of 1967.

For 1964, Tonka began a program to diversify its facilities and products. The year started with an agreement with the Mercury Tool and Stamping Company in Toronto, Canada, to manufacture and distribute Tonka Toys under a licensed agreement. This marked the beginning of Tonka's worldwide expansion. Before the year was

NO. 739 — AL
like the big m
on the highwa
to the weight
cavernous int
house full of
doors make lo
be detached fro
and van. 24¼"
wide. Packed 4
30 lbs.

1963 No. 308 Stake Pickup.
Dennis David

85

Profile
Lowell Fritzke

Lowell Fritzke had just been released from the service in 1960 when a friend of his mentioned that Tonka was looking for help. He went there the next day, got a job, and worked for Tonka until 1991. "I had no idea when I started that I would be there for the next 31 years, but that's how it was there. The people were like family, and you didn't want to leave," he said. Throughout his years with Tonka, Fritzke moved up in the company and eventually became distribution manager. "Tonka paid for me to go to school, and because of that, I was able to have a wonderful career," Fritzke said.

Fritzke was one of the few employees to make the move to Juarez, Mexico, before production was moved, and he remembers it was like stepping into a different world. "The pace was much slower, and for a while it was hard to get anything done," he said. Fritzke opened Tonka's Juarez facility, and he vividly remembers dealing with Mexico's industrial infrastructure. "I had a phone in my car, which was rather unusual in those days, and it was basically my office because we couldn't get the phones installed." At the time, Sylvania was building a plant across the street from Tonka, and the plant manager came over one day and proudly announced that he had phone service. "I asked him how he got it, and he said he had talked to the Minister of Phone Service down in Mexico City." The next day, Fritzke took a ride down to see the official and saw several Sylvania television sets lined up against the wall of the office. "I learned how to do business in Mexico that day," he said. There were also problems with power failures. "We were the first company in Mexico to do plastic injection molding, and the power would go out two or three times per day, which wreaked havoc with the plastic because it would harden up inside the machine," he said.

Fritzke spent several years at the Juarez facility and returned to Mound to work at Tonka's corporate headquarters. Fritzke now works for a Minneapolis firm and travels to China extensively, but his years spent at Tonka will always be a big part of his life. "Tonka gave me many opportunities, and for that I will always be grateful."

out, Tonka acquired the Mell Manufacturing Company in Chicago, Illinois. Mell built outdoor barbecue grills, which fit in nicely with Tonka's plans for diversification, as the grills could be manufactured during the seasonal downtime of the toy business. All of Mell's equipment and machines were moved to Mound, and by January 1965, Tonka manufactured and sold grills under the Firebowl label. The Firebowl had a short-lived tenure at Tonka because the toy business became busy enough to warrant year-round production. Tonka also purchased a huge press, which employees called the "Minster Monster," that was able to punch out the barbecue bowls with ease.

The successful Mini-Tonka line featuring the Jeep Gladiator–style pickup was carried over for 1964 with limited changes. New colors, decals, and a plated grille gave the line a fresh look. There were a few additions to the line when Tonka introduced several construction models. A new addition to the Mini line was the No. 76 Road Grader. In keeping with the Mini line's respect to scale, it had a single axle on the rear instead of the double on Tonka's larger Road Grader. The Mini Road Grader was very successful for Tonka and remained in production with only decal changes until 1972.

A cement mixer based on the Mini line was also featured in 1963. This toy is extremely unusual for Tonka in that it was actually introduced midyear. The introduction of a toy midyear during the 1960s was virtually unheard of at Tonka. Despite the introduction, there is a unique difference between years as the crank handle was moved from the right to left side for 1964. Built on the standard Gladiator chassis, the No. 77 featured a tilt-back mixer that was riveted to the rear frame. The drum turned by a crank handle on the side that turned a set of gears. The mixer was finished in red with white molded plastic parts.

Tonka also introduced a new style in 1964 that closely followed American culture. After President Kennedy's space exploration challenge in the early 1960s, many toy companies took hold of the concept of space travel. A look back at toys from the 1960s shows a fascinating array of rockets, lunar rovers, and launch pads. As a manufacturer of toy trucks, Tonka needed a way into this market, and the Futuristic Cab design was born. With a radical front windshield that ran from its roof to its front bumper, the Futuristic design demonstrated that Tonka was ready to embrace the future. Some collectors refer to this design as the telephone booth cab.

No. 404 Farm Stake.
Dennis David

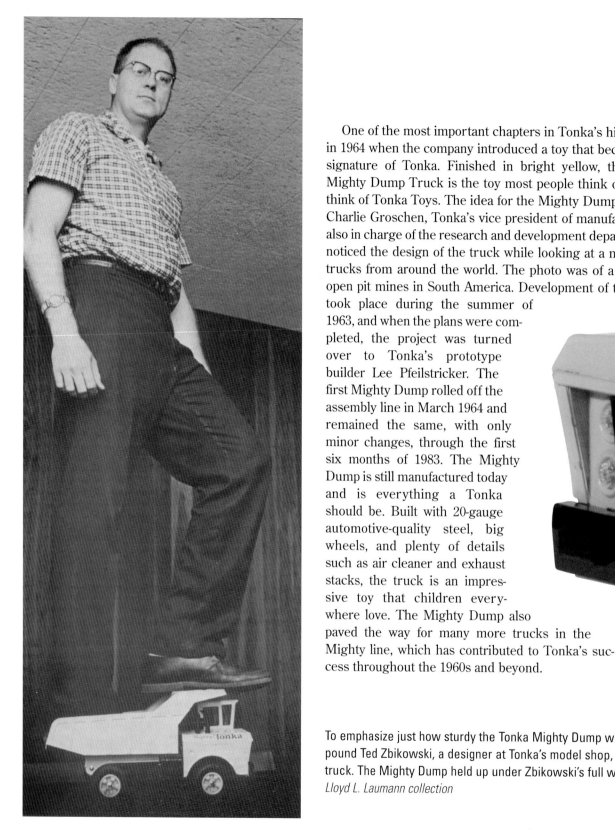

One of the most important chapters in Tonka's history happened in 1964 when the company introduced a toy that became the very signature of Tonka. Finished in bright yellow, the No. 900 Mighty Dump Truck is the toy most people think of when they think of Tonka Toys. The idea for the Mighty Dump was credited to Charlie Groschen, Tonka's vice president of manufacturing, who was also in charge of the research and development department. Groschen noticed the design of the truck while looking at a magazine featuring trucks from around the world. The photo was of a truck used in the open pit mines in South America. Development of the Mighty Dump took place during the summer of 1963, and when the plans were completed, the project was turned over to Tonka's prototype builder Lee Pfeilstricker. The first Mighty Dump rolled off the assembly line in March 1964 and remained the same, with only minor changes, through the first six months of 1983. The Mighty Dump is still manufactured today and is everything a Tonka should be. Built with 20-gauge automotive-quality steel, big wheels, and plenty of details such as air cleaner and exhaust stacks, the truck is an impressive toy that children everywhere love. The Mighty Dump also paved the way for many more trucks in the Mighty line, which has contributed to Tonka's success throughout the 1960s and beyond.

To emphasize just how sturdy the Tonka Mighty Dump was, 240-pound Ted Zbikowski, a designer at Tonka's model shop, stood on the truck. The Mighty Dump held up under Zbikowski's full weight just fine. *Lloyd L. Laumann collection*

1965 No. 2900 Mighty Tonka Dump
Mark A. Vaught collection, Lee Klancher

Profile
Evelyn Stephens

Evelyn Stephens applied for a job at Tonka in 1960. "I needed a new washing machine and a dryer, and I figured I could buy it by working at Tonka." She worked at Tonka for 23 years and loved every minute of it. "The people were so nice, and it really was like having a great big family." Evelyn started out on the assembly line, but she then moved over to the janitorial crew. "I walked 23 miles per day on my cleaning rounds," she said, referring to the huge Mound, Minnesota, plant. She also worked with the tour-guide department, which consisted of uniformed women who gave tours of the entire plant. "We started at the cutting line and then showed them the production line, the paint line, the dip tanks, assembly, and then on to the packaging area." Although the tour was a long walk, Evelyn couldn't recall anyone ever complaining.

Evelyn was Tonka's unofficial poet, and she wrote hundreds of poems for employees' birthdays and other special occasions. She still has her scrapbook, which is filled with poems describing many different events that occurred at Tonka over the years. Although she retired from Tonka in 1981, Evelyn keeps busy and is involved with many local charities. She often goes to garage sales and picks up clothing for needy families. Occasionally, she comes across a Tonka toy and buys it for some lucky child. "Tonka toys were built to last, and even if it's not shiny anymore, a child can still have fun with it."

1965 No. 2 900 Mighty Dump
Mark A. Vaught collection, Lee Klancher

By the mid-1960s, American culture had changed dramatically. The 1950s were a distant memory, and the decade of turmoil was upon the nation. With a large opposition movement to the Vietnam War in full swing, Tonka suffered a decline in sales of its military line of toys. Tonka was now a completely different company from the early days; it was now a corporate giant. Products under Tonka's holdings featured the Firebowl barbecues, and the company acquired Gresen, a manufacturer of hydraulic valves. Expansion and modernization of Tonka's toy manufacturing facilities increased output to an astounding 8,000,000 toys, which exceeded the combined output of the American automobile industry. Tonka had truly become the largest builder of toy trucks in the world.

The Minster Monster in action.
Gordon Batdorf collection

Fast Fact

THE MINSTER MONSTER

As a manufacturer that was on the cutting edge of new technology, Tonka was always looking for the newest and best equipment. The purchase of the "Minster Monster" was a unique acquisition for Tonka. Among one of the largest presses available from Minster at the time, the Minster was purchased solely to increase production of the Firebowl barbecue.

Manufactured in Minster, Ohio, the press was unique thanks to its 45-degree angle. The reason for the angle was that gravity allowed the barbecue parts to fall away. On the assembly line for smaller toy parts, Tonka usually used air pressure to move parts along, but the weight and size of the barbecue parts was too great for this method. Previous to acquiring the Minster, Tonka's production used the tooling purchased from Mell and made one barbecue per minute. The piece had to be removed from the press by hand. The Minster punched the bowls out at a rate of 30 per minute, which increased production and reduced costs.

The press was truly a monster. Weighing in at 110,000 pounds, it was built especially for Tonka, and there was only one other like it in the United States at the time. It was moved to Mound on a railcar at a cost of $6,000, and its immense size and weight mandated that it needed special treatment. It was moved on the flatbed railcar only during daylight hours and never at more than 30 miles per hour. It also had to stay off the main lines, and its trip to Mound was a meandering route from Ohio to Minnesota.

The Minster was an incredible piece of machinery that was capable of forming large pieces of steel. It was only fitting that the world's largest producer of pressed-steel trucks would have one of the biggest presses available. The Minster was sold when production ceased at the Mound plant, and with it went another piece of Tonka's history.

Chapter 8
1965–1969

BY 1966, TONKA'S EMPLOYMENT HAD GROWN TO OVER 1,000 PEOPLE, AND THE COMPANY manufactured toy trucks at a rate that was unmatched by any toy company in history. While Tonka was certainly communicating with the world and getting the word out about its products, employees were stretched across the huge facility and sometimes were not aware of changes in the company. Wenkstern, Batdorf, and Groschen guided the day-to-day operations, but there were so many employees that communicating with all of them was difficult. In March, a new publication for Tonka employees was launched. *Tonka Today* was a bimonthly newsletter to make all Tonka employees aware of happenings in and out of the plant. In the first issue, Russ Wenkstern was quoted as saying, "The name of this new publication, *Tonka Today*, pretty well sums up its reason for its being started; we need something to keep us all informed of what's going on here at Tonka, and in touch with one another. *Tonka Today* is intended to accomplish that important task."

Although *Tonka Today* was a publication intended for employees, a look through any of the issues gave employees valuable insight into the manufacturing plant and American society. Tonka's business and its employees were always the main subjects of the newsletter, and the insight provided by its contents provided a look into American history. New hires, births,

1966 No. 304 Jeep Commander (minus the roof support).
Dennis David

An aerial photo of the Mound plant in 1967.

Lloyd L. Laumann collection

deaths, marriages, new appointments, and bowling scores from the company league were all chronicled in *Tonka Today*. Today, these newsletters are very scarce and it's rare that one is even seen, let alone sold on the open market. The newsletters prove beyond a doubt that Tonka went out of its way to make employees content and create a work environment that was both fun and productive. Tonka management recognized its people as its most important asset.

Tonka had reached the very pinnacle of its manufacturing capabilities in 1966. The company operated out of 503,000 square feet of floor space. The expansions and upgrades had added a research and development room, a new tool room, an employee cafeteria, and medical facilities. Tonka's plant was a model of efficiency, thanks to its commitment to machinery upgrades and employee involvement. Although the company had begun 20 years earlier in a small schoolhouse, it was recognized as one of the finest metal-fabricating facilities in the Midwest.

Tonka had experienced phenomenal growth since its inception, but there was still an air of trust and sincerity within the work force. Tonka's employees were not unionized, which removed many barriers when introducing new products and changing assembly lines. For 1966, employees manufactured a total of $15,138,380 worth of toys; add to that another $4,407,933 worth of Firebowl barbecues, and the commitment of Tonka's employees becomes evident. Sales data suggested that Tonka's toy vehicles were still seen as Christmas presents because 66.7 percent of Tonka's shipments for 1966 occurred between August 1 and December 10. Through all of the growth and expansion, the suggested retail price for a Tonka dump truck had not changed since the very first model in 1949. At $3.98, the look of Tonka's dump truck had changed considerably, but the price had remained the same.

There were now three different sizes available in the 1966 Tonka lineup. The Mini line was very successful, and the regular size was still a favorite with children everywhere. The new Mighty line laid the foundation for incredible sales, and in a few years, this line alone defined the very name of Tonka. A grand total of 61 toys in various sizes and sets were featured for 1966, and another six accessory bagged sets sold as "To Play Toys" were also offered.

One of Tonka's semi trucks that were used to haul shipments across the nation. Circa 1967.
Lloyd L. Laumann collection

"Working With Friends"

Tonka

TONKA CORPORATION
MOUND, MINN. 55364
PHONE: 612-472-2431

Lloyd Laum

EMPLOYEE HAND BOOK

5.5 Be a Regular Attender — Build a Good Attendance Record

Tonka needs your services every day. If you are ill and unable to report for work, notify the Company Nurse or Personnel as soon as possible and always before starting time. If you are unable to report to work due to compelling personal reasons, notify the Personnel Department before starting time. Personnel, or the Nurse, will inform your supervisor. If an employee is frequently tardy or absent, an extra burden is thrown upon his fellow workers. A good attendance record and promptness will work in your favor when promotions are available.

5.6 Keep Your Work Area Clean and in Good Order

Good housekeeping promotes good workmanship and safety. It is your responsibility to have your tools and work area neat and orderly at all times and especially at the end of the day.

5.7 Be Helpful

Help us make a good impression on all of our visitors. Many of them are customers or prospective customers. All visitors must be identified by "Visitor" badges which they receive at the reception desk. A "Visitor" badge indicates that the wearer is a customer, government representative, salesman, repairman or other visitor.

5.8 Termination Notice

If you have to quit, we ask that you give Tonka at least two weeks notice.

Tonka's policies can change from time to time and we will try to keep you informed if any changes occur.

WE ARE VERY PLEASED TO HAVE YOU
ON OUR TONKA TEAM ! ! !

Tonka employee handbook from 1967.
Lloyd L. Laumann collection

Although limited production originally began at the old schoolhouse in 1946, Tonka observed its 20th anniversary in 1967. The logic behind this was that 1947 was the year that regular manufacturing started. Tonka manufactured over 10 million toys in 1967, and total corporate sales reached $31,852,273, which included sales of Firebowl barbecues and Gresen hydraulic products. Although Tonka's holdings weren't completely diversified, they turned in some impressive profits. Volkswagens, Mini pickups, and the Mighty Dump carried the bulk of toy sales. Fifty-eight models were offered for the year, and Tonka dropped 20 models from the previous year's lineup. The No. 62 Jeep Wagoneer, No. 88 Van, No. 90 Livestock Van, No. 402 Air Force Ambulance, and several others that didn't move off the retailers' shelves were discontinued.

On January 2, 1968, the production lines at Tonka roared back to life and built toys for the 1968 model year after a two-week hiatus. For the first time in its history, Tonka shut the lines down on December 15 of the previous year and began the next year's production immediately after the first of the year. In earlier years, all lines were shut down in late November or early December, and production of new models didn't start until March. The conversion from seasonal to year-round production occurred because Tonka now had a wide array of toys at all price levels. New and more sophisticated forecasting and scheduling techniques were also implemented, and this allowed for smooth production. Sales and marketing strategies were designed to encourage early orders and maintain a steady flow of orders throughout the year. Tonka reaped the full benefits of an expanded line of products, and Tonka had a toy for every parent's wallet.

An important change to Tonka's management was made in 1968. Tonka's corporate headquarters were moved away from the Mound plant. Space was leased on the second story of an office building located west of Minneapolis to allow Tonka's corporate management to focus on the company's business without day-to-day involvement at the manufacturing facilities. The purpose of relocating corporate management was to provide more focus on anticipated expansion and diversification. Plans were developed for extensive expansion and relocation of corporate management, and as a result, additional layers of management were added to train Tonka management for future manufacturing and distribution facilities. These decisions were excessive for the future market potential, and a major reorganization of management happened in 1971. The levels of management were reduced, employee accessibility to management was increased, and future market potential was re-evaluated.

The introduction of the Mini line in 1963 was highly successful, and the addition of the Mighty line in 1965 added a good balance to the higher-end toys. Although the two lines and the regular Tonka line were very successful, they paled in comparison to what was

Behind our Four Big Frontliners...

...are

in store for 1968. The addition of the Tiny-Tonka resulted in the most profitable year since the beginning of the company. The Tiny line vehicles sold for $0.99 and took the toy industry by storm. Manufacturing at the Tonka plant was so intense that the company was forced to sell the Firebowl barbecue line in order to devote all of its resources to toys. Tonka also increased ownership of its Canadian subsidiary from 75 percent to 100 percent, and it added a 123,000-square-foot addition to its Malton, Ontario, facility. In a continuation of its worldwide expansion, Tonka acquired a 39 percent interest in its Auckland, New Zealand, affiliate.

The first of nine Tiny-Tonkas introduced for the year was the No. 515 Pickup. The design was loosely based on the Ford Motor Company's Econoline Pickup, and other subsequent trucks in the Tiny line were built on the same platform. A dump, wrecker, fire truck, cement mixer, garbage truck, and a van followed the first

A 1969 promotional flyer for Playthings.
Lloyd L. Laumann collection

98

rd-Hitting Linebackers!

When your line is Number One in the Steel Truck League, naturally you want to keep it there. That's why ours is backed by strong advertising, merchandising and promotion programs. It means there's plenty of interference out front when you carry the ball for Tonka. With this kind of support, there's far less chance to get tossed for a loss. And a far better chance to break loose for long gains. Carry Tonka and follow your blockers to paydirt.

ADVERTISING LINEBACKERS

Colorful tv commercials break through to the kid market.

Three tv commercials, all in color, will blitz through to millions of kids across the nation. There's one on Tiny-Tonka, one on Mini and Regular Tonka and another on Mighty-Tonka. Each is a full 60-second play-action spot, designed to create instant replay with live Tonka Toys.

There's also a sustained drive at parents.

In this League, you can't neglect the parents. We don't. Full color advertisements will appear in both Good Housekeeping and Parents' magazines. Often enough to make millions of moms cheer for our side (and yours).

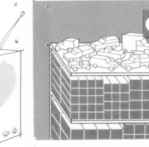

Plus a little book with big sell-power.

Every youngster that gets a Tonka Toy gets the Tonka Look Book. It shows our full line in full color with a strong message directed at parents. Object: repeat sales! This year, 25,000,000 will be printed and inserted in our toy packages.

Free materials to quarterback your own advertising.

It's easy to call the plays on your own Tonka Toy promotions. We provide everything you need free: Reproduction photographs (color and black and white), complete with item descriptions and newspaper ad mats with illustration and sell copy. Available for every toy in our line. See your Tonka Representative about our advertising allowance.

MERCHANDISING LINEBACKE[RS]

Free Display Kits make big impact play.

Here are point-of-purchase materials that hit 'em with impact. Kits spell out the Tonkas you offer like the color cards in the home team rooting section. Contains a big Tonka oval with stand, Tiny, Mini, Regular and Mighty-Tonka gondola signs, gummed labels for out-of-package identification plus a Tonka oval decal. Free.

Manual provides coaching on how to build winning displays.

Free from us or your Tonka rep, this book diagrams effective gondola displays so simply that even rookie stockboys can understand. It's invaluable as a display-building primer as well as a handy reference for keeping displays properly stocked.

Packaging as colorful (and attractive) as pompom girls.

Tonka Toy packaging is designed to tell everything it's possible to tell on a package. What the toy inside is. What it looks like. Its color. Its size. Packages also provide effective merchandising and protection for toys.

Long range sign power.

When this big 4-ft. Tonka trademark hangs suspended, it leaves absolutely no doubt in the customer's mind where the Tonkas are.

1968 Pickup.
Dennis David

Tiny-Tonka pickup. The original design of the Tiny-Tonka cab was so successful that it did not change until 1982.

Tonka's regular line received a new cab design in 1968. Many collectors refer to this cab style as the Dodge-style cab due to its resemblance to Chrysler's style of trucks during the 1970s. This cab carried more detail than any other Tonka cab had yet produced. The doors featured embossed, simulated door handles, and the dashboard had two embossed raised panels with simulated gauges and a glove box. There were plastic seats and a clear plastic cab insert that enclosed the cab's windows. The new style featured the Tonka name in the center of the grille. The design of this cab was so successful that it wasn't changed until 1977. This cab also represents the last of Tonka's true steel trucks because a new design in 1978 significantly increased the plastic content.

By 1969, Tonka was now a worldwide leader in the toy industry, and it seemed an entire culture had grown with the company. Employees at Tonka were referred to as "Tonkans" in *Tonka Today*. Many wonderful moments were captured on the pages of *Tonka Today*, and if it wasn't for this newsletter, these moments would be forever lost to time. A photo in the August 1969 issue shows a group of women from the night shift calmly playing cards after they were directed to the shipping area while a tornado passed through. Another article in the October issue has a photo and accompanying story of Ethel Yost, who won first place at the Meeker County Fair for the tablecloth that she crocheted. Any employee achievement that was deemed newsworthy found its way onto the pages of *Tonka Today*.

Tonka experienced something new in 1969 when a dip in profits caused some concern. Management's primary focus during the 1960s had usually been product development and growth management. For the first six months of 1969, sales were $17.5 million, at an increase of nearly $2 million, but earnings did not increase for the first time since Tonka

1965 V-Stores Special Van.
Lee Klancher

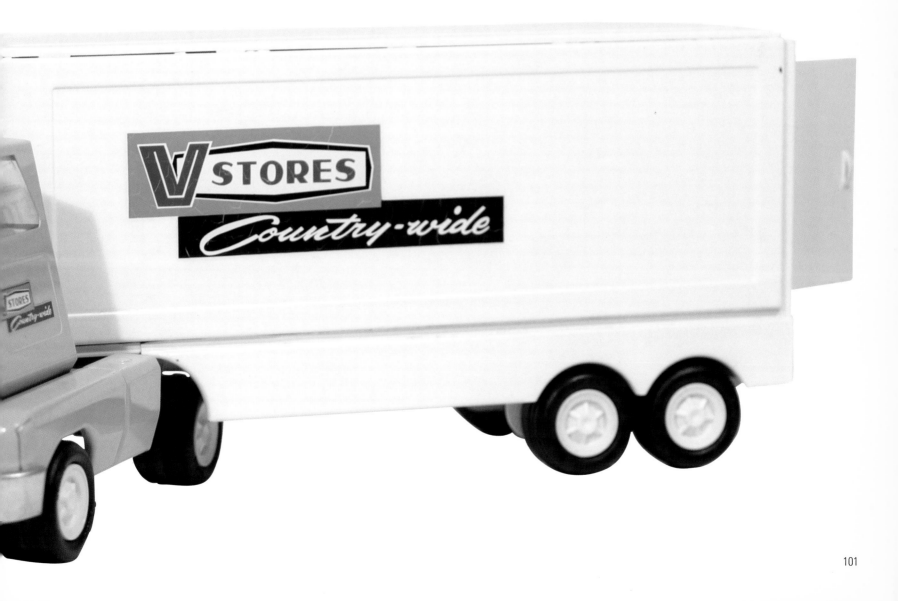

Tonka plaque from 1968.
Dennis David

went public in 1961. After-tax earnings through June 28, 1967, were $713,476, which was $22,474 below the previous year. While it was a concern, it didn't immediately sound the alarm bells. It would take more bad news to shake the company into a new plan that would ultimately make or break the future of Mound's largest employer.

On August 18, 1969, Gordon Batdorf resigned. Since joining the company in 1946, Batdorf rose through the ranks and had been involved in the expansion of Tonka from a small company at the little schoolhouse to the largest manufacturer of pressed-steel toys in the world. Batdorf continued to serve on Tonka's board of directors, and Russ Wenkstern assumed Batdorf's responsibilities. The August issue of *Tonka*

1968 Tiny Sanitary.
Dennis David

Profile

Ralph J. Ehalt

While there are several million people who can say that they played with Tonka trucks while growing up, Ralph Ehalt can say that he actually drove a Tonka truck. As a delivery driver in Tonka's fleet of tractor-trailers, Ehalt spent 21 years hauling Tonka's products throughout the United States and Canada. "When I started driving for Tonka in 1963, we were running Macks, Diamond Ts, and Whites, and they weren't like the beauty queens seen on America's highways today," Ehalt said. By the time Ehalt left the company in 1984, Tonka used Peterbilts and Kenworths. "Trucking has come a long way since the 1960s," he said.

Ehalt says that Tonka's truck runs could last anywhere from a few days to more than a week. "We ran two-man teams on the West Coast runs because they were long, but the eastern runs to New York or Chicago could be done in a few days by one man." Tonka's trucks weren't empty when they returned to Mound. "We usually hauled produce back from the West Coast, and plastics or metal back from the East Coast," he said. Ehalt and the rest of the Tonka fleet hauled most of the inventory out of the Mound plant when production moved in 1983. "That was a sad day because a lot of good people lost their jobs," Ehalt said.

Driving a real Tonka tractor-trailer was exciting, but not without its unusual moments. "Cars would pass our trucks with kids pressing their noses against the glass while begging parents to maneuver the car for a better look," Ehalt said. While he spent most of his time on the road, Ehalt remembers Tonka with great fondness. "There were some really nice people there, and the truck maintenance crews were really good, they took really good care of the trucks."

Today quotes Wenkstern as saying, "We regret Gordon's decision to resign, but we feel fortunate that his talents will still be available to us as a director on the Board."

Tonka's products for 1969 featured an incredible array of 86 models. Research and development was hard at work as nearly one-third of the 1969 lineup were new or restyled toys. Toy sales in the United States reached $2 billion, and Tonka outpaced the competition by wide margins. From 1964 to 1969, toy industry sales in general increased by 58 percent, while Tonka's rate of growth outpaced the toy industry with sales increases of 140 percent. Tonka became the giant

1969 Dump Truck.
Dennis David

Profile

Gordon Batdorf

When Mound Metalcraft founder Lynn Baker removed himself from the day-to-day operations of Tonka Toys in 1961, Gordon Batdorf was elected vice president and treasurer. Over the next decade, Tonka Toys saw continual growth that resulted in one of the country's largest toy companies.

As a returning World War II pilot of a P-47 Thunderbolt, Batdorf initially sought work as an airline pilot. Unfortunately, no one was hiring pilots with single-engine experience, so Batdorf enrolled in the Academy of Accounting in Minneapolis. He was very good at accounting and was hired by Avery Crounse at Mound Metalcraft. "Although my accounting experience was zero, Mr. Crounse recognized that I could do the job and hired me on the spot," Batdorf said. Batdorf rose rapidly in the company. He became president in 1964 and guided Tonka's growth through acquisitions and new products until his resignation in August 1969. "Those were some good years at Tonka, and I think we were good at what we did."

After Batdorf left Tonka, he formed the consulting firm Batdorf, Blair & Associates. Several years later, after he served on the board for three years, he was brought in as president of Larson Industries to restructure the failing boat company. The company filed bankruptcy, but Batdorf helped turn the company around.

Although now in his 80s, Batdorf still enjoys the challenge of business and is currently leading Renaissance Fertilizers Inc., a company specializing in organic fertilizer. Batdorf has no intention of slowing down or retiring. He still has the same drive and determination he had during his years at Tonka. "I love working, and business is my life."

1965 Road Grader.
Dennis David

of the toy industry, and its products were in most households across the United States. The company's presence was felt around the world with distributor and/or manufacturing capabilities in Canada, the United Kingdom, West Germany, France, Italy, Holland, Switzerland, Austria, Ireland, and Sweden. Products for these countries were shipped directly from Tonka's Canadian plant. With a new decade just around the corner, it would seem that Tonka was poised to do even greater things, but trouble was waiting with the new year, and it would take the efforts of everyone at Tonka to maintain the company's position in the toy industry.

Russell Wenkstern in 1968.
Lloyd L. Laumann collection

Fast Fact

THE MIGHTY DUMP

When most people think of Tonka, they immediately think of the No. 900 Mighty Dump Truck. Introduced in 1964, the big yellow truck was created to give the appearance of brute strength. The Mighty Dump's unique design has held up well over the years, and although it has completely changed, it is still part of the Tonka line.

The genesis of the Mighty Dump began with Tonka's management, who felt there was a need for a line of larger-sized trucks. Charlie Groschen, head of Tonka's research and development, looked around at some of the various construction companies in the Mound area and found the Cox Brothers yard in Spring Park, Minnesota. The Cox Brothers supplied Groschen with a few construction equipment magazines, and he came across a picture of a truck used in the open pit mines of South America. Groschen took the picture back to the plant, and Lee Pfeilstricker built a prototype of the truck. The design was shown to Tonka's management, and everyone liked its look. Work on the tooling started immediately, and production began a year later. Yellow was chosen as the color because of its predominance in the construction industry. The Mighty Tonka Dump was changed only when an improvement could be made, but it mostly stayed the same until 1983. To figure out how many Mighty Dumps were built over the years, Groschen estimates that it took about 15 minutes to assemble a Mighty Dump on the assembly line at the Mound plant, and the line ran daily for many years. "The last I heard it was about 25 million," he said.

The Mighty Dump is tough because it was designed and built to be the toughest toy truck in the world. Testing for the truck was harsh. It was subjected to extreme heat, freezing temperatures, and loaded with 35 pounds of weight and run on a conveyor belt for 400 miles. The harshest test may have come from children, who routinely sat in it and rode down driveways and hills.

The type of truck that served as the model for the famous Mighty Dump is not that easy to figure out. "It's hard to say really," Charles Groschen said in a 2004 interview. "The magazine that I was reading when I got the idea for it was written in Spanish, and I never found out what it said!" The Mighty Dump bears a strong resemblance to several models manufactured by Euclid, Terex, and General Motors. As far as the original prototype built by Lee Pfeilstricker, "I think we lost it in the press room," said Groschen. At the time, no one knew it was going to be the most successful toy truck in history. Needless to say, if the prototype was still around, it would probably be the most valuable toy in existence.

Chapter 9
1970–1974

TONKA OFFERED 113 MODELS FOR 1970, A YEAR THAT WAS DIFFICULT FOR THE TOY INDUSTRY. A national recession took hold of the U.S. economy, and Tonka's sales declined to $27,002,000.Production also declined. For 1970, Tonka's employment peaked at 1,526, a number far below the 1,991 employees for 1969. Before the year was over, the work-force number was trimmed with layoffs in October. A letter from Tonka personnel director Lou Jones printed in the October 1970 issue of *Tonka Today* explained that orders from retailers were not forthcoming, and Tonka had no choice but to reduce the work force. Jones also emphasized that the layoffs were temporary, the 1971 product line had already been approved, and the company was optimistic about better times ahead.

In December 1969, Tonka began manufacturing a new line of toys based on the Tiny line. Known as "Crazy A's," the line featured five different hot rods of modified Ford Model A's. With names like Frantic Flivver, Mod Rod, Stinger, Scorcher, and Draggin Wagon, children everywhere could not get enough of the cars. The Crazy A's were purposely introduced after the 1969 Christmas season in order to bolster sales during this normally slow period. The line was so successful that another four models were introduced at the 1970 March Toy Fair.

1970 No. 2850 Car Carrier.
Dennis David

The Crazy "A" assembly line in 1970.
Lloyd L. Laumann collection

The success of the Crazy A's led to the development of the Tonka "T's," which were a variation on Ford's famous Model T. Highly detailed and very durable, the Tonka T's were very successful in the Tonka lineup for 1971.

Several agreements were forged in 1970 that were truly unique in the toy industry. In an agreement with the Pillsbury Company, Tonka entered a test program that put Tonka's toys on the shelves of grocery stores. The thought at the time was that toy sales in grocery stores was an untapped market, and the two-year agreement included several research and development studies that gauged the effectiveness of these sales. The program did not meet either party's expectations and was eventually dropped. Another agreement in 1970 produced huge profits for Tonka. In an agreement with Bandai, a major Japanese toy company,

negotiated by Russ Wenkstern, the two companies formed a joint venture with a goal to produce and market toys internationally. The name of the new venture was Tonka Japan, and this subsidiary held the exclusive sales rights of Tonka products in Japan and other Asian countries. With headquarters in Tokyo, parts and products were supplied by Tonka's Canadian and New Zealand factories, and some parts came from the Mound, Minnesota, plant. In return for Tonka products for the Asian market, Japan Tonka held the exclusive rights to export Bandai's products to the United Kingdom, Canada, New Zealand, and Australia. Tonka's marketing organization distributed Bandai's products, and the agreement worked well for both companies. In a gesture toward the new international agreement, the Tonka logo changed in 1970. The words "Mound, Minn" below the wavy line were replaced with "U.S.A." Any child that played with a Tonka toy anywhere in the world would know where it was built. The design of this logo remained until 1973.

A look back on Tonka's year for 1970 produces some interesting observations. The company experienced nothing but expansion and growth all through the 1960s, so why did 1970 prove to be such a hard year financially? Many Tonka historians suggested the company was overexpanded and had too many layers of management in the early 1970s. Tonka had become such a large company that running the business was no longer a simple proposition. While the early days in the schoolhouse may have been devoted to new products and increasing market share, the early 1970s demanded more attention to personnel issues, productivity, and survival in a market with strong competition. These internal pressures, combined with the external pressures of a recession, acted together to make a difficult business year for Tonka.

Logo from 1970 to 1973.
Lloyd L. Laumann collection

Logo from 1974 and 1975.
Lloyd L. Laumann collection

Although the Tonka line offered many toys in different sizes, there was room for another addition. Tonka started development and production for a new concept called Tonka Totes. These extremely small vehicles were built with a stainless steel undercarriage and used axles engineered for minimum friction. There were eight different styles, and all used a body crafted from a high-impact polycarbonate. Accessories for the Tote line consisted of a launcher- and ramp-style turnaround, which offered hours of playtime fun. A close inspection of one of Tonka's Totes reveals their similarities to Mattel's Hot Wheels cars. Unfortunately, the timing was not right for Tonka's entrance into this market. Style and color changes were made to Tonka Totes during the three years they were built, but they were not as successful as the company had hoped. They remain a rare collectible in today's market.

Ceramichrome bisque kits were sold through Tonka in 1974.
Lloyd L. Laumann collection

Another new Tonka toy for 1970 capitalized on NASA's Apollo space flights and man's conquest of the moon. The Crater Crawler was a four-wheeled vehicle that featured oversized tires borrowed from the Mighty line, an articulated hinge point in the body, and a clear plastic dome over the driver's seat. It featured Celestial Blue plastic components, off-white tires, and white steel components, and it was an impressive toy that was able to handle the roughest terrain with ease.

Another new addition for 1970 was the No. 1045 Ruff Rider. The impetus for this off-road vehicle came directly from the rugged woods of Minnesota. Many Tonka employees loved the great outdoors, and the Ruff Rider's design was patterned from the all-terrain vehicles that some Tonka employees owned. The underside of the Ruff Rider was steel, while the upper was plastic

molded in Apple Green. The toy featured six wheels and molded plastic seats. There was even a simulated gearshift and dashboard. Finding a Ruff Rider today is a difficult task because they were built only from 1970 to 1973.

In 1969, the Consumer Product Safety Commission, a division of the Federal Food and Drug Administration, enacted the Federal Toy Safety Act. This act was meant to enhance the safety of toys made in the United States. Compliance with the act was not voluntary, and its ramifications directly affected the entire toy industry. The renewed focus on safety showed up in Tonka's line for 1971. All models had to be deburred, new hemmed edges appeared on many models, finger entrapments were eliminated, nonshatter materials were used on windshields, and Tonka's toys continued to be finished with nontoxic paints and inks. While these mandates changed the look

1968 No. 555 Wrecker
from the Tiny line.
Lee Klancher

of many toys, they did not diminish the quality, and Tonka's line featured an impressive array of 137 offerings for 1971. Management changes were also made in 1971 as Dale R. Olseth was named president and chief operating officer after Russell Wenkstern resigned. Olseth is credited with bringing diversification to the Tonka line, and Wenkstern remained on the board as chairman and delegated responsibilities to Olseth while Wenkstern prepared for his retirement in 1977. Troubled times persisted for Tonka in 1971, and toy sales declined to $25,986,600. Consumers kept their money in their pockets due to economic uncertainty, and employment at Tonka for 1971 decreased to a dismal 1,221 employees, the lowest in five years. Despite the bad news, Tonka ended 1971 on a profitable note with net earnings of $0.95 per share.

A new line, the "Scramblers," was introduced in 1971. These toys were unique for Tonka because they used a friction-powered motor that enabled them to speed across the floor. The friction motor for the Scrambler was engaged by pressing down on the toy and moving it forward. This wound the spring-driven mechanism, and when the pressure was released, the Scrambler sped across the floor. The Scrambler line was manufactured by Bandai for Tonka's U.S. market, and eight models were introduced. With names like Hub Heater, Lightnin' Rod, Wind Burner, Hot Horse, and Ground Pounder, the Scramblers were successful and remained in the Tonka lineup for five years.

Additions were made to the Tote line for 1971, including some very stylish racers. A dragster-based model called the Strip Whip featured huge exhaust headers and big tires, and

1977 No. 947 Shell Tanker.
Lee Klancher

1973 Hoerner Waldorf Special
Lloyd L. Laumann collection

another new model, Beach Buzzer, was described in promotional material as the "clown prince of the drag strip." A highly detailed rear engine and big headlights gave the Buzzer a radical look. The Totes line was very successful for 1971, and Tonka said good-bye to the Jeep Gladiator, which had generated huge profits for Tonka since its inception in 1963. The Jeep Gladiator style in the Mini line was abandoned and completely redesigned for 1971. It was replaced with a radical new cab called the Super Thrust. This forward-looking cabover truck featured an expansive windshield and a one-piece bumper and grille with a futuristic look. The design was well received and stayed with selective Tonka models until 1980.

The company faced tough times, and an attempt was made to minimize costs. Tonka began to eliminate a few details from their toys. The saddle fuel tanks were eliminated on the No. 3902 Hydraulic Dump and the No. 3900 Mighty Dump in order to reduce cost and

1970 No. 3920 Mighty Tonka Loader.
Dennis David

maintain its price in retail stores. Many details in other lines were also removed, and collectors today tend to focus exclusively on Tonka's pre-1972 period due to the amount of detail in its toys.

Tonka's silver anniversary was in 1972, and after two years of declining profits, a turnaround was in the works. Management spent many hours during 1971 trying to figure out what Tonka's problems were, and a planned direction for the company emerged from these meetings. Broadening the products and reorganizing on a worldwide level were the major concerns identified. The Gresen Hydraulic Valve Company expanded with a new manufacturing facility in the works and began penetrating foreign markets. Tonka also announced an agreement to acquire Vogue Dolls in Melrose, Massachusetts, in October 1971. The deal

Left to right: Dale Olseth, Russell Wenkstern, and Ted Nelson are pictured in February 1973 when the company acquired Vogue Dolls. Olseth is handing Nelson a stock certificate.
Lloyd L. Laumann collection

1973 No. 3885 Mighty Tonka Winnebago.
Lee Klancher

1973 No. 3885 Mighty Tonka Winnebago.
Lee Klancher

was completed, and dolls manufactured with Tonka's logo appeared in January 1973. Another agreement with Winnebago Industries allowed Tonka to build a beautiful motor home. This toy was built in the Mighty line, billed as the flagship of the 1973 lineup, and marketed to both boys and girls who loved it for its size and detail. The girls admired its removable top and smart interior layout that featured realistic furniture. The boys liked the flat roof, which was easy to sit on while riding down the driveway.

For 1973, it appeared that the tough times at Tonka were beginning to brighten. Corporate sales rose to $83,413,727, and the Mound, Minnesota, facility alone manufactured and sold $48,258,270 worth of Tonka toys. Employment stood at 1,575 people, and the increase in sales resulted in the purchase of a vacant 300,000-square-foot building owned by the J. R. Clark Company in Spring Park, Minnesota. Located two miles from the Mound plant, the warehouse became the distribution center for Tonka's products.

Tonka's toys for 1973 were now more diverse than ever. The company was no longer just a manufacturer of toy trucks, and it built everything from campers to hot rods. The company weeded out several lines that didn't sell well. Tonka Totes were dropped, but the Tonka Toddler's line was expanded to eight models for 1973. A new product within the Gigglers line called Peek-A-Boo People was introduced to young children. The Peek-A-Boo toys were small, and their facial expressions changed as their caps were rotated. They also could fit on the end of a small finger to act as puppets. Finished in bright and stimulating colors, the Peek-A-Boo line had their own set of vehicles. Another addition for 1973 was the Tonka Scorcher line. These ultramodern-looking vehicles used the Torque Thrust friction motors, which were common in Tonka's products in the early 1970s. Recreational vehicles were also in demand as Ski-Doo and Arctic Cat snowmobiles were featured in the Action line. The No. 800 Mini-Winnie was also introduced for this year. This small camper provided children with hours of fun on the open road. This vast array of product offerings demonstrates how far Tonka had to go to remain competitive in the toy market.

1972 Camper.
Dennis David

Profile
Don Hilgers

Don Hilgers joined Tonka in 1963 at the age of 18. He had just graduated from high school, and Tonka paid for his night school to become a master of the tool-and-die trade. It took six years, and he went on to a rewarding career with Tonka. "It was a great place to work, and we really had some great times there," he said. Hilgers remembers the company managers coming in on Saturdays to help out. "That's the way it was there—everyone pitched in to get the job done."

Hilgers remembers the process that Tonka took to create a new toy. "We'd make up a model from metal or wood, then it would be reviewed and a decision would be made on whether or not it would be built." Tonka had a special room in another building that was used to store the prototype toys that weren't selected for the final cut. "Sometimes they would turn a certain design down and it would wind up on the shelf of that room, but they would go back a few years later and pull it off the shelf and put it into production." There is no doubt that modern-day collectors of Tonka would pay handsomely for some of the prototypes that were in that room, but according to Hilgers, "I don't know what they ever did with all that stuff!" Hilgers said that he and his coworkers had to build new dies for the Mighty Tonka Dump Truck at least four times. "Most of the products we built sold really good at first, and then died off, but the Mighty Dump just kept on going."

Hilgers continued to build custom designs for Tonka after production left Mound, Minnesota, and he worked at the new facility in Texas for a short time. He said it was a completely different world down there. "In Mound, the women were the backbone of Tonka's production, and it took quite a few people in the new plant to equal the productivity that Tonka had in Mound." Hilgers doesn't regret a single minute he spent working for Tonka. "Working at Tonka was like being a part of a big family, and I'm proud to have been a part of it."

1973 No. 2315 Dump Truck.
Dennis David

A significant milestone was reached in 1974 as Tonka Corporation's sales exceeded the $100 million level. Total sales volume was an astounding $102.1 million, with $72.6 million of that from the toy division. The new distribution center was up and running, and Tonka had a new method of promotion with a direct-sales force. Employment levels were the highest in Tonka's history with 2,026 people. Big changes were made to the product line for 1974 when 59 models were dropped from the previous year. This was offset by the introduction of 39 new models, with a total of 112 models for 1974.

Tonka experimented with different paints in the early 1970s. Prior to 1970, Dupont was the sole supplier of paints for Tonka's products, but the company experimented with paints made by Glidden, Valspar, and Dexter-Midland. Paints were supplied by several different companies on a regular basis. While certain toy lines usually received the same color from the same manufacturer, there were variations, which is why many of Tonka's products during this period have color inconsistencies. The use of multiple paint suppliers continued

1973 No. 2545 ERV.
Dennis David

1970 No. 1045 Mini Tonka Ruff Rider
Dennis David

through the early 1990s. Tonka once again changed its logo in 1974 when the "U.S.A." below the wavy line was dropped.

Tonka introduced an innovative new toy in 1974 when an alliance was formed with the Smithsonian Institution. These toys, Tonka Dioramas, were sanctioned by the museum and had an educational appeal. The dioramas were hobby toys that required assembly and featured prominent moments in American history. Tonka's initial offering of the Diorama line consisted of four different models that were all featured in highly detailed form: Charles Lindbergh's landing in Paris, Henry Ford's Model T, the Pioneer Locomotive, and the Wright Brothers' first flight. The dioramas were a unique offering from Tonka because they differed greatly from the pressed-steel toy truck line.

Tonka survived hard economic times in the early 1970s, but by the middle of the decade, the company emerged stronger and more diversified with its products. Tonka's line was now so expansive that a child could literally grow up with Tonka's products. The Peek-A-Boo line could provide a child's first toy, while the Mighty line could still entice boys well into their teens. Tonka captured the heart and spirit of America, and its products were purchased by parents who remembered playing with Tonka's toys themselves some years earlier. The Good Housekeeping Seal, *Parents* Magazine, and Steel logo were now printed on Tonka's packaging, and Tonka's quality was a recognized standard in the toy industry.

As Tonka worked through 1974, President Dale Olseth announced a new operating structure for the company. A new three-division plan was enacted, and its primary purpose was to meet continued growth requirements. The toy division encompassed Tonka Toys U.S.A. and all other toy manufacturers around the globe. The Hydraulic Division consisted of Gresen valves, and the Hobby-Craft Division managed Tonka's educational products and the Ceramichrome Inc. ceramic coatings line. The divisional structure enabled Tonka to be proactive in its growth, and each division could now receive the attention it deserved. These changes helped Tonka meet the future with a degree of certainty that it didn't have when it was heading into the 1970s, and the company was poised to experience an increase in profits.

Fast Fact

TONKA'S TRUCK FLEET

It would seem fitting that a company that built toy trucks would have a few real trucks around the plant. Although Tonka's fleet of delivery trucks was small by industry standards, each one of the company's over-the-road trucks averaged thousands of miles per year. Tonka's fleet for 1979 stood at 15 tractors, with one switcher for yard work, and four pickup trucks. Each tractor-trailer covered anywhere between 1,000 and 4,800 miles per trip, and there were four departments in the trucking division. The first was the local delivery department that handled anything from mail drops around the plant to trips to Tonka's Spring Park warehouse. The second and third were the East and West divisions that handled deliveries to both coasts of the United States, and the fourth division was maintenance.

The eastern division trucks were driven by one man, while the western division ran two-man crews in trucks equipped with sleeper cabs. The western trucks averaged 4,200 miles per trip and were constantly on the move. The trucks were maintained a few blocks from the Mound manufacturing facility. Tonka also had its own training program that allowed drivers to gradually work their way up from local deliveries in small pickups to big cabover trucks that used 13 forward gears. Although turnover in the trucking industry was always a problem, Tonka never had any trouble keeping good people because drivers worked out schedules between themselves and regularly alternated the short and long trips.

So what did Tonka's trucks haul back after delivering their load of toys? Many hauled raw materials to the Mound facility, and others took on contract work for other companies in the Twin Cities area. Western trucks hauled back fresh produce for Super Valu grocery stores. Even though the Tonka name may have been proudly displayed on the side of the trailer, there was no guarantee that it wasn't hauling lettuce, raw steel, or plastics.

Chapter 10

1975–1979

By 1975, Tonka had become a global giant with facilities scattered throughout the world. Company operations were located in Australia, Belgium, Canada, France, Japan, Netherlands, United Kingdom, United States, and West Germany. The divisionalization streamlined the company's operating structure, and this made the organization more efficient. For 1975, corporate sales were $97 million with $56 million coming from U.S. toy sales. The Mound plant employed 2,026 people, and although Tonka was now a giant corporation, the people of Mound were still the backbone of the toy-manufacturing operation. The Tonka name generated excellent toy sales, but the Gresen Division produced handsome profits as well. Tonka's new Vogue Doll line featured a new "Wash-A-Baby" doll for 1975, and the Ceramichrome line of stain and glaze products for ceramics, as well as the Tonka Diorama sets, sold well. Diversification was clearly the key to survival in a market with strong competition. Although Tonka spent many of its years on the forefront of the toy industry, it faced stiff competition from companies such as Ideal, Mattel, Hasbro, Parker Brothers, and Fisher-Price.

1979 Tiny Bell Truck.
Dennis David

Tonka employee appreciation dinner
in November 1978.
Lloyd L. Laumann collection

Tonka was presented with the coveted Clio Award for "World's Best Live Action 30 Second Commercial" in 1975 for a commercial developed by Carl Ally Advertising. In the commercial, a huge elephant named Nellie placed its body weight on a Mighty Tonka Dump Truck. The impetus for the commercial came from various explanations for children breaking their toys. One child's excuse of "an elephant stepped on it" gave the ad agency the idea, and the commercial was born. The commercial ran during 1975, and it effectively demonstrated the strength and durability of Tonka's products because the toy didn't break under the elephant's weight.

Tonka introduced 107 models at the New York Toy Fair in February 1975. A separate showroom adjacent to the main Tonka display featured the Vogue Doll line, which was operated as a separate division and manufactured in Melrose, Massachusetts, and Franconia, New Hampshire. Four new additions were made to the Smithsonian Diorama lineup, primarily to stimulate diorama sales. Although Tonka had five fewer models in the total lineup than in the previous year's lineup, 23 of 1975's offerings were all new, and Tonka's packaging allowed prospective buyers to actually see the product through a cutout on the front panel. Each toy's action was described on the back panel, and a triangular-shaped red panel in the upper left-hand corner featured the word "Tonka" in large white letters. Tonka's packaging had bold and vibrant colors that brightened the aisles of toy stores everywhere.

Vogue Doll catalog.
Lloyd L. Laumann collection

vogue *1975*

NEW PRODUCT Vogue introduces a number of exciting new dolls to the 1975 product line. These introductions offer something new for every age level; new 12" & 16" Wash-A-Bye-Baby series, new 15" Miss Ginny Contemporaries and several new additions to the already popular 8" Miss Ginny Collector series. *VOGUE'S UNEXCELLED RECORD FOR SERVICE ASSURES PROMPT AND EFFICIENT BUYER DELIVERY ON ALL PRODUCTS.*

SKIN TONES & HAIR STYLES Vogue knows that the more "lifelike" a doll the more loveable she is to a little girl. Softer-looking, more colorful and more "alive" faces een on our dolls this year. Some of our hair styles and colors will be changing a bit too, oftly-fashioned waves, beautifully straight and flowing and we even have some ponytails.

NEW CONTEMPORARY CLOTHING Vogue has created several new clothing designs reflecting today's fashions and ideas. One of our young ladies wears an embroidered denim outfit, another, a stylish suede-like pant suit. "Today" dolls, for today's little girls.

IONWIDE DIRECT SALES FORCE Vogue Dolls are sold exclusively s National Direct sales force.

vogue dolls
Tonka

New Packaging for '75!

☆ Designed to provide total VOGUE LINE identity for maximum shelf impact.

☆ Purchase-motivating sales copy and graphics.

☆ Structurally designed for improved physical package strength and product visibility.

When Tonka introduced the No. 101 Golf Cart in 1960, it was met with little success. Various parts of it were used on the No. 720 Airport Tug, which also had limited success. A new addition to the Tiny Tonka line in 1975 evened the score a bit with the No. 995 Tractor and Stake Wagon. The nifty design had a detachable wagon. Despite the failure of Tonka's tractors in the early 1960s, the No. 995 generated profitable sales.

Tonka dusted off the dies from a previous line and retooled for the No. 1986 Nostalgic T Set that was also introduced at the New York Toy Show in 1975. Using the dies from the hot rod T toys produced from 1971 to 1973, the nostalgic T recreated an authentic- and original-looking Model T that was appealing to both children and antique-car collectors. The line consisted of a milk truck, a pickup, and a roadster. Contrary to the hot rod look of Tonka's T's a few years earlier, these toys featured narrow tires and correct fenders. After dropping the Mini Tonka Military Jeep from its line in 1969, Tonka introduced the No. 1989 Military Jeep as a new model. After several years of lagging interest, military toys gained favor. Tonka marketed a military set in 1975 that consisted of a Jeep, a loader, and a pickup. Tonka's sales strategy for the mid-1970s was an intense effort to reach consumers by offering a variety of different models.

1978 No. 2635 Shell Tanker.
Lee Klancher

Change was the word as Tonka entered the 1976 toy season. Peter M. Winsatt was appointed president and replaced Dale Olseth. The Vogue Doll line was sold, and Tonka closed its West German distribution subsidiary. Toy division's sales were down 2.8 percent from the previous year, and a restructuring throughout the company attempted to reverse the declining sales. Employment at the Mound plant totaled 1,901 people. A new logo was used on all models for 1976. The oval now contained a bright red background with "Tonka" spelled out in white letters. A white border surrounded the oval, and the wavy line that signified the waters of Lake Minnetonka was eliminated. Because Tonka offered such a vast array of toys, they marketed new toys by combining several existing products. The No. 1971 Landscape Truck & Loader is one example of this new product method. The truck was a newer version of Tonka's No. 1245 Super Thrust Crate, and the loader was the No. 581 Tiny Tonka Tractor with a loader attached to it. Mixing and matching various models enabled Tonka to create sets that kept the product line fresh for every new toy season.

Peter Wimsatt.
Lloyd L. Laumann collection

1977 No. 147 Mite Dump.
Lee Klancher

Cover of the 1977 annual report. Clockwise from top: Peter Wimsatt, John Hohenshelt, Charles Weinschreider, and Wayne Nelson.
Lloyd L. Laumann collection

On the other side of the scale, the large Mighty Tonkas sold well and required only minor changes for 1976. The Tonka logo decal was eliminated above the grille on the No. 3900 Mighty Dump, and the No. 3907 Mighty Dozer was painted Ocher. Color changes also affected the No. 3915 Mighty Wrecker when light blue and white replaced orange and white. The success of the Mighty line carried Tonka through many tough times, and a redesign eventually came, but for now, there was no need to drastically alter its style.

On November 1, 1977, Tonka's chairman of the board Russ Wenkstern retired, which closed a big chapter in Tonka's history. Wenkstern was among the last of the original management team, and it was now up to a new generation of people to carry the Tonka name forward. Wenkstern's unique ability to bring people and ideas together for a common cause contributed directly to the success of Tonka throughout his tenure. Of the many employees interviewed for this book, all expressed an admiration for Wenkstern that is seldom seen in American business. While Wenkstern may have officially retired, there was one more chapter for him to write in Tonka's history. In 1984, Tonka senior vice president Pat Feely consulted with Wenkstern on a Japanese venture for Tonka. Wenkstern built a good relationship with the Japanese, and his open and friendly manner assisted the negotiations.

Profile
Peter Wimsatt

Peter Wimsatt was hired as a production control manager in 1969. In the next several years, he climbed the company ladder and advanced to vice president and head of domestic operations, and then to president of Tonka Toys. As Tonka's leader, Wimsatt initiated several changes during his tenure, and his business expertise guided Tonka through some very interesting years.

As vice president and general manager, Wimsatt was part of the team that eliminated the representative sales force and instituted direct sales, a move that cut costs and enabled customers to have direct contact with Tonka's sales force. Wimsatt also instituted another policy that had executives work on the production floor. "I always believed that management should spend at least one shift in every department on both the day- and night-shift production floor—that way you really found out what doing someone's job was all about," he said. Wimsatt recalled working on a rivet machine on a night shift and having trouble. "The woman who ran the machine told me I wasn't going to make my quota for the shift and laughed."

Wimsatt has a great fondness for Russ Wenkstern. "Russ was just a great guy that everybody really loved." He recalled an incident with Russ when the two of them were walking the factory floor and a woman on a forklift gave Russ a great big smile. Russ immediately gave her a pat on the back, and when he walked away, the woman turned to Wimsatt and said, "Watch him—he's going to jump up and click his heels." She was right.

Wimsatt still has a few Tonka Toys around, including a commemorative chrome-plated Mighty Dump Truck. Wimsatt left Tonka in 1978 to pursue other interests, but he remembers his years at Tonka with pride. "Those were some really good years at Tonka, and because of the people, it was a great place to work."

With the departure of the old guard, Tonka hired several new employees in various marketing-related management positions, and the company was poised for new growth. With a new generation at the helm, Tonka found new highs, but the seeds of controversy were planted as the way was paved for Tonka's eventual exit from the Mound area. The people hired at Tonka during the late 1970s may have thought that they had a job for life, just as their mothers and fathers had. The harsh reality proved to be different. In a business world that constantly searched for new ways to improve profitability, Tonka took steps to streamline operations in any way it could. One of Tonka's largest operating costs was its work force, which was paid well by industry standards. The employees were extremely bright and resourceful people that had a genuine love and commitment to the company they had grown up with. In a few short years, the cost of Tonka's work force became a critical factor in the company's plans.

The No. 3985 Mighty Tonka Custom Van debuted in 1977. It featured an open top and sliding doors and measured an incredibly large 18 5/8-inches long. The van was available in copper or blue, but both versions used a two-tone brown and beige interior. A scenic mural decal was affixed to both sides of each model, and children everywhere could explore the wonders of the open road. Another new offering in the Mighty line was the No. 3986 Adventure Buggy. This toy was marketed in the spirit of adventure, but its docile appearance spoke directly to girls. Not since the introduction of the No. 350 pink Jeep Surrey in 1962 had Tonka captured the imagination of girls. The rugged Adventure was an attempt to recapture that market once again, and it happened to be just the right size for Mattel's Barbie and Ken dolls.

Significant changes occurred at Tonka in 1978. The entire Tonka line was given a fresh new look, and the company was in the midst of more management changes. Many Tonka historians referred to this period in the company's history as the "executive revolving door" era since there were newly hired division and corporate officers every year. The previous year, Charles J. Weinschreider was installed as executive vice president of the corporation and toy division on April 4. Weinschreider brought 13 years of experience from the Fisher-Price Toy Division of the Quaker Oaks Company, and Tonka's products were greatly influenced by his efforts. Another management change occurred on December 5, 1978, as Peter M. Wimsatt resigned as chief executive officer and chairman of the board. Wimsatt also resigned as director of the corporation and effectively ended his tenure at Tonka. Pending the election of a new chief executive officer, an operating committee consisting of the company's board of directors managed the company. Board member Stephen G. Shank was designated to act on behalf of the operating committee as acting chief executive officer and chairman of the board while a search was conducted for a new replacement. After six months, the committee interviewed several candidates, but none met the criteria. The committee then decided to appoint Shank to both positions, which he assumed on March 21, 1979.

1978 No. 2585 Hydraulic Dump.
Lee Klancher

Weinschreider's influence was felt almost immediately with major changes to the 1978 product line. A grand total of 168 different model toys were marketed, which was the largest number in Tonka's history. There were new bold and vibrant colors, and packaging was changed again and allowed consumers to see even more of the product before the purchase. The colorful appearance of Tonka's products was the result of a close association with paint suppliers Dupont and Glidden. This association also produced some of the most durable paint finishes in the toy industry. Paints were applied by electro-disposition, rinsed, dried, sprayed with another coat, and baked for a hard, vibrant finish.

The famous Tonka logo underwent its most radical change in 1978. The familiar oval was dropped, and the word "Tonka" was in its place. The "T" connected with the "K" and created a line over the "O" and "N." This logo carried Tonka into the new millennium and beyond. These changes signified the end of the original design created back in 1946. The "T" and "K" had been joined in 1962.

Tonka began 1979 on a high note, and the outlook for orders was excellent. This was because many of Tonka's retail stores were completely sold out in 1978. The new colors and refreshed packaging had done their job, and Tonka looked forward to filling the store shelves with its 1979 models. Orders were up significantly at the European Toy Fairs as well, and Tonka's expansive toy line offered products for children of every age. Confidence was high, and with a successful previous year, many employees looked forward to an even better year. The Mound plant was an industrial giant with activity consuming every corner of the

Logo from 1976 and 1977.
Lloyd L. Laumann collection

Logo from 1978 to 1991.
Lloyd L. Laumann collection

building. The Spring Park warehouse served as Tonka's main distribution center. Only Henry Ford's Model T rivaled the generation of so many products in one location and production at an incredible volume that involved the efforts of all employees. Tonka made improvements to everything from research and development to production. Among the changes was a new method for building wheels on the Compact and Mini lines. Previously, Tonka's wheels for these lines were a labor intensive two-piece wheel and hub assembly. The new process used a hot stamp method to manufacture a one-piece wheel. Output was increased significantly with 25,000 wheels per eight-hour shift for the Mini and Compact lines. These impressive numbers allowed Tonka to cut costs and increase productivity.

Many changes were in store for Tonka as the corporation crossed into the 1980s. Manufacturing operations at the Mound plant were nothing short of incredible. The plant was almost like a city in itself with medical attention available when needed and a kitchen capable of feeding hundreds of people on a daily basis. Overall, the future looked bright, but little did anyone know that in a few short years, the Tonka name would find a new home, and production at the Mound, Minnesota, plant would come to an end.

Fast Fact

MARKET RESEARCH

In Tonka's early years, product design was created in-house, and reaction was gauged by feedback from toy fairs. By 1978, Tonka's forecasting was much more sophisticated, and the company created its own marketing and research department that handled such tasks as analysis of sales data, relation of actual to potential volume of new products, testing new commodities, and monitoring advertising and sales promotion efforts and the attitudes of consumers and dealers toward Tonka's products. While the department worked for Tonka, their scope sometimes involved how customers viewed competitors' products as well.

Instead of creating a toy and hoping it would sell, Tonka's marketing and research department provided management with an objective estimate of volume potential of a new product early in the development phase, which helped identify the potential sales volume of its toys. The department also provided valuable data regarding who would buy a product, how it would be used, and what consumers liked and disliked about a product. Tonka's management also received reports at regular intervals, including a monthly store sales report. This reported the sales and inventory from selected discount and toy stores from all over the nation, which was analyzed for trends on prices, themes, and sales performance.

The ultimate goal of the market and research department was to correctly anticipate consumers' needs before they occurred. This enabled the company to accurately coordinate new product introductions that were specifically timed for the market. There were many other factors that figured prominently into the sales equation; lifestyles, economic trends, and demographic forecasts were all studied by the department. These studies and analyses enabled Tonka to accurately gauge the needs of consumers.

7.000.000ᵀᴴ MIGHTY DUMP
MANUFACTURED
8:11 A.M.– MAY 3, 1982

Chapter 11

1980–1983

RUSS WENKSTERN WANTED TO RETIRE IN THE LATE 1970S, SO HE SPENT SEVERAL YEARS PERSONALLY selecting the people for Tonka's second generation of management. His aim was to leave Tonka in the hands of people who shared his own management philosophy. The departure of Dale R. Olseth and Peter M. Wimsatt led to the third generation of management, and although the offices of president and chief executive officer remained constant from March of 1979 until 1991, other management positions changed regularly. Many employees referred to this era as the "executive revolving door."

The Tonka toy division returned to profitability in 1979 with sales of $93 million, an increase of 26 percent from 1978. Operating profits reached $9 million, and Tonka's products were well received, especially in the U.S. and Canadian markets. There was a certain degree of uncertainty regarding the ownership of Tonka's stock in 1980, and this was cleared up in March of that year. On March 3, Tonka Corporation reached an agreement with Mego International Inc., its subsidiaries Mego Corporation and RMCPM Inc., and Bramah Incorporated. The agreement called for Bramah, an inactive United States–based subsidiary of Bramah Limited of England, to purchase 314,000 shares of common stock owned by Mego. This transaction represented 20.1 percent of Tonka's stock, and the deal ended Mego's attempted takeover of Tonka. Gordon Bramah, Bramah's chairman of the board, was elected to the Tonka board of directors.

The seven millionth Mighty Dump (No. 3900), built in 1982.
Dennis David

The seven millionth Mighty Dump rolled off the assembly line at 8:11 a.m. on May 3, 1982. Pictured here are Gary Graham, department manager; Helen Slanga, Doris Splettsoeszer, and Melinda Johnson, department supervisors.

Lloyd L. Laumann collection

In an effort to streamline operations and focus Tonka's business plan on building toys, the company sold its Gresen Valve division. On January 1, 1981, Tonka president and CEO Stephen G. Shank announced the sale of Gresen Manufacturing Company to the Dana Corporation of Toledo, Ohio, for $37,500,000 in cash. Gresen had provided Tonka with many years of good profits, but Tonka wanted to focus on dominating the global toy market.

Tonka made another attempt to capture the preschool market with the introduction of a new line of toys. The Rainbow Top, Bear in the Box, Snap Mates, Tot-A-Phone, Toddler Talkies, Stackable Shapes, Stack-N-Rings, and Scrub Boat toys were aimed directly at young children and introduced them to the Tonka brand name at an early age. Riding toys were also added in 1981, which went on to become highly successful. In 1980, Tonka also introduced the largest pickup truck ever made by the company. The Mighty Roughneck Pickup had some unusual features for a Tonka. It had four removable tires and came with a heavy-duty jack and spare tire. It also featured a play figure named "Big Duke" who fit inside the pickup. This toy represented the largest investment ever made by Tonka in a new toy. Sales expectations were high with 405,563 pickups sold in 1980, but despite the fact that the toy was marketed in three different versions in 1981, sales fell to 164,982 units and consumers were unable to justify the cost. Tonka's expanded offerings to the toy market also included the introduction of the Hand Command Turbo Prop Airplane, and the use of A. J. Foyt's name in the Builder's Play Sets. Tonka attempted to market toys of all shapes, sizes, and prices to cover the wide spectrum of the toy market.

With the sale of Gresen, Tonka was able to focus its efforts entirely on the toy division. Management was aware that foreign competition was a threat to Tonka's very existence. With this in mind, John Hohenshelt, Tonka's vice president of operations, advised employees that the company was considering manufacturing some of the smaller toys in Mexico. Tonka employees did not initially express a big concern over this announcement, but a short time later Tonka announced the construction of a new 73,000-square-foot manufacturing facility in Juarez, Mexico. The anticipated completion date was in March, and production was set begin soon after.

A licensing agreement between Tonka and Elkay Industries in 1981 represented a new frontier for Tonka. The agreement called for the Tonka name to appear on a line of children's apparel designed by Skyline Industries. This was the first of many nontoy licensing agreements that Tonka entered into, which generated profits for the company. Tonka licensed many of its products in the 1980s, which enabled the Tonka name to be displayed on everything from lunch boxes to clothing.

Tonka was a company that had been identified with Mound, Minnesota. Even its early name, Mound Metalcraft, invoked the spirit and inspiration of its namesake. On October 27, 1982, it was announced that Tonka would close the Mound, Minnesota, plant and move all manufacturing to El Paso, Texas, and Juarez, Mexico. Labor costs, taxes, and proximity to the West Coast markets were cited as the major factors to this decision. Tonka's corporate and toy division headquarters remained in Minnesota and employed 150 people. Tonka pledged to handle the closing in an equitable and considerate manner for employees, who expressed sadness and bitterness at the reality of losing their jobs. The decision to move to Texas had actually been made two months earlier when Tonka president Steven Shank hired a consulting firm that concluded Tonka's survival in the global toy market was directly related to cutting costs.

The phase-down of manufacturing operations at Mound began soon after the announcement, and several lines headed to El Paso and Juarez. The move continued through 1983, and by the end of the year, production at the Mound facility had ceased. The last day of production was December 9, 1983, and Tonka's Hard Hat was the last product to come from the Mound facility. With the mighty machines of the Mound

Tonka continued on page 12A

BN continued on page 12A

The lead story for the October 28, 1982, edition of the Minneapolis *Star and Tribune* was of Tonka's relocation. *Lloyd L. Laumann collection*

Construction of Juarez, Mexico, Tonka Plant in 1981.

Gary Campbell

Gary Campbell remembers the day he started work at Tonka because the day turned into a week. "It was March, and I went in on a Monday and a major snowstorm hit. We ended up stranded at the plant, and I never made it home until Friday," he said. Fortunately for Campbell and a few others that were with him, there were beds in the nurse's station they could sleep on, so it wasn't too bad. "That's the way it was at Tonka—we always worked things out and found a way to get the job done."

Campbell spent the next 19 years working in the press room, and although there were only a few machines when he started in 1965, the department grew quickly and was soon home to several large presses with power measuring 250-ton capacity. Campbell remembers the famous Minster Monster that Tonka bought to punch out its Firebowl barbeques. "It was huge, and the power it had was incredible," he said.

Campbell was one of the last employees to leave the Mound plant as he helped load equipment that was sent to the El Paso and Juarez plants. "The big presses were moved by professionals because of their immense size and weight, but we loaded all of the personal things like desks, chairs, and tables onto trucks where it went south from there." Campbell admits he had a sinking feeling every time he loaded up another piece of Tonka's history. "It was really sad when Tonka left Mound because so many good people worked there, and I knew it would never be the same." As a skilled press operator, Campbell found work at another factory in the Winsted, Minnesota, area, and he is still there. "I'm sure that if Tonka did not leave Mound, I'd still be there today. It really was a good place to work, and the people were like family."

plant now silenced, the employees and citizens of Mound reflected on the toy giant that had once called their town home. Throughout the years, the Tonka Toy Company had accumulated some incredible statistics. Among them were:

- At peak production, 1,500 employees produced approximately 325,000 toys per week.
- More than 12,500 tons of 20-gauge automotive grade steel were used each year, which is enough to build 19,500 automobiles.
- The Tonka press room punched out over 1 million stampings each week.
- Tonka used more than 50,000 gallons of nontoxic paint annually. This was enough paint to cover 10,000 houses.
- Tonka manufactured over 60 million toy tires each year.
- Over 12 million pounds of plastic were processed each year at the Mound plant.

The very last issue of *Tonka Today* was a difficult issue for employees to read. Tonka president Steven Shank expressed his appreciation to the Mound employees for the manner in which they performed their jobs throughout a difficult year. The same issue carried a letter from vice president of manufacturing, Lloyd Lauman, who recognized Tonka's employees as the company's greatest asset. His letter stated that, *"Tonka management has and will continue to appreciate that we have been truly blessed with good people in Minnesota. I am both humbled and honored to have had the gratifying opportunity to meet, know, and work with some of the best people in the world."*

With Tonka's manufacturing facility in Mound now closed, the mighty industrial machines that had made millions of toys were gone. After beginning life in a small schoolhouse with the vision of three very different men and growing into one of the largest toy producers in the world, the Tonka name moved away. The silence throughout Mound was as eerie as the ice-covered waters of Lake Minnetonka.

Laura Smith, the group leader for the division, and the seven millionth Mighty Dump.
Lloyd L. Laumann collection

Fast Fact

RETRAINING

When Tonka announced it was going to leave Mound, many employees openly wept at the harsh reality of losing their jobs. It came as a shock to many, as very few of the employees knew that a move was in the works. The first reference of the move in *Tonka Today* wasn't until the December 1982 issue. The last issue of *Tonka Today* was printed in December 1983.

While production wound down in preparation for the move to Texas, Tonka helped its employees find new jobs. Meetings were immediately held with the Hennepin County Employment Training Program representatives, the director of the Comprehensive Employment and Training Act Services Department, and the military. Meetings with the governor and the state's congressional representatives were also held to help Tonka's employees find new jobs and bring manufacturing contracts to the Mound area.

Tonka employees immediately filled out questionnaires that determined their strengths and assessed their skills. During this time, many questions were asked regarding health benefits, pensions, retraining, and the end of production. Job workshops were held throughout the year, and although there were other employers in the Mound area, there was no way to fully absorb all of Tonka's employees into other companies. Tonka was Mound's largest employer. Through all of Tonka's darkest hours in 1983, employees continued to do what they did best—they made toys.

Chapter 12

1983–1991

ON APRIL 21, 1983, TONKA TOYS MOVED OFF THE ASSEMBLY LINES IN EL PASO, AND BY THE BEGINNING of 1984, production was well underway. Tonka was moving toward becoming a different company. A heavy emphasis on promotion of its products around the world took the company to new highs in market penetration. While Tonka had always been known as a builder of pressed-steel trucks, a renewed effort in the diversification of its products brought incredible success. With production no longer located in Mound, Minnesota, a new era for Tonka was being built. In May 1984, Tonka introduced a new company newsletter called the *Tonka Corporate Report*. This newsletter featured articles from Tonka's divisions around the world, and an explanation of the publication's parameters appeared in the very first issue.

"The Tonka Corporate Report will be business oriented. Social or individual accomplishments or articles only will be included if they impact the business."

While the original publication known as *Tonka Today* mixed Tonka news with news of many of the people who worked there, the *Tonka Corporate Report* was a business-only newsletter.

1989 No. 3901 commemorative silver powder-coated Mighty Dump manufactured in El Paso, Texas.
Dennis David

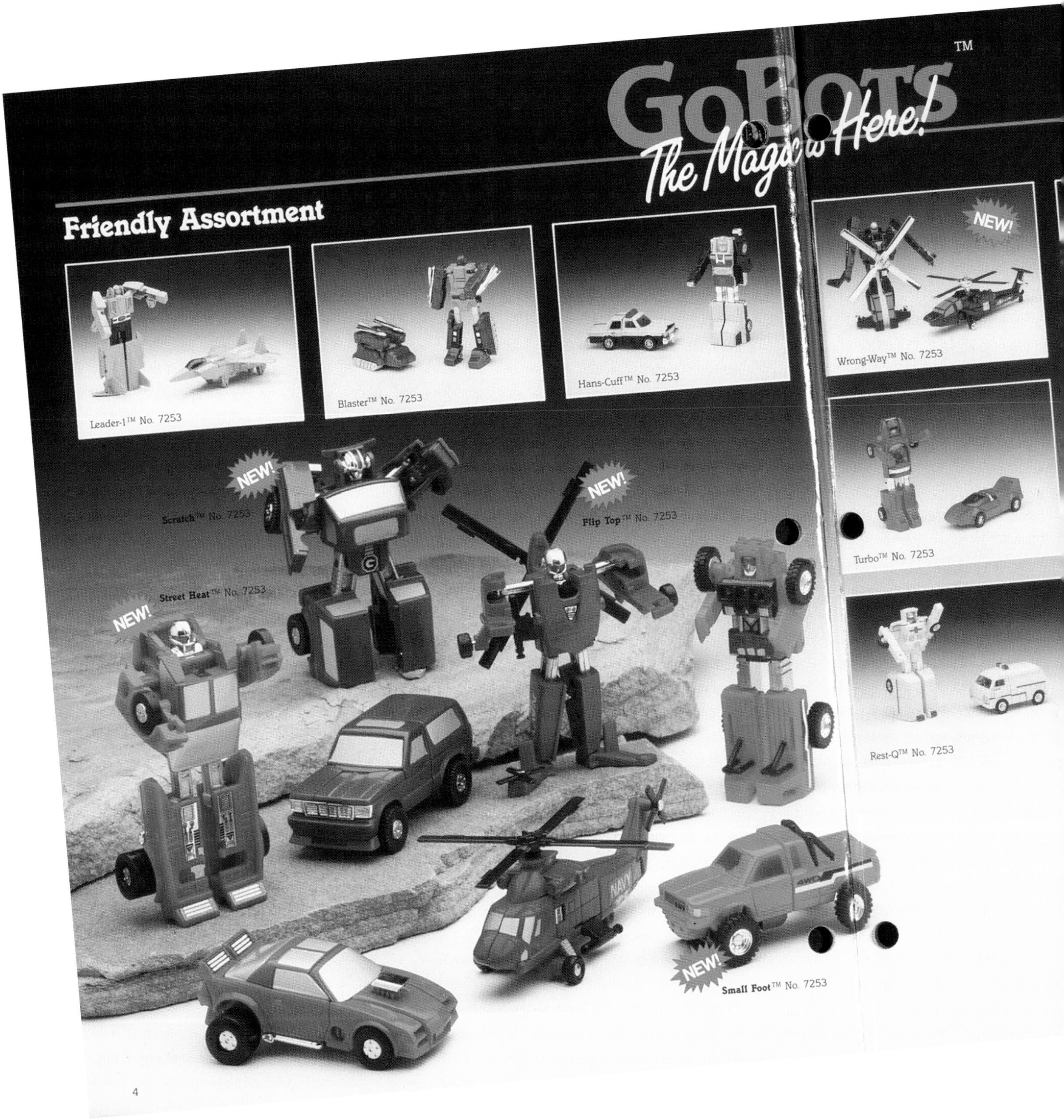

Friendly Assortment

Leader-1™ No. 7253

Blaster™ No. 7253

Hans-Cuff™ No. 7253

Wrong-Way™ No. 7253 **NEW!**

Scratch™ No. 7253 **NEW!**

Flip Top™ No. 7253 **NEW!**

Street Heat™ No. 7253 **NEW!**

Turbo™ No. 7253

Rest-Q™ No. 7253

Small Foot™ No. 7253 **NEW!**

Good Knight™ No. 7253

No. 7253

NEW!

er™ No. 7253

Spay-C™ No. 7253

NEW!

NEW!

ve™ No. 7253

Van Guard™ No. 7253

e planet GoBotron™, the GoBot invasion
continues. With good and evil locked
al combat, the fate of millions hangs in
ance.

1, Friendly Robot Leader, has called for
nal help in the battle against Cy-Kill and
emy GoBot conspirators. New Friendly
s arrive in droves to aid their fearless

dly GoBot Asst. I No. 7253
ghty Robots that turn into Mighty Vehicles!
-cast metal and high-impact plastic design

rtment includes:
er-1 Friendly Robot Leader
o Friendly Robot Racer

Hans-Cuff Friendly Robot Police Car
Flip Top Friendly Robot Helicopter
Good Knight Friendly Robot Car
Dive-Dive Friendly Robot Submarine
Small Foot Friendly Robot 4 x 4 Truck
Spay-C Friendly Robot Space Ship
Rest-Q Friendly Robot Ambulance
Pathfinder Friendly Robot UFO
Blaster Friendly Robot Rocket Launcher
Street Heat Friendly Robot Street Machine
Wrong-Way Friendly Robot Attack Copter
Scratch Friendly Robot 4 x 4 Truck
Van Guard Friendly Robot Mini Van
Heat Seeker Friendly Robot Fighter Plane

Ages: 5 and up
Master Pack: 48

5

One of the first Tonka products to real-
ize profits with the diversification effort
was the GoBot. Introduced in 1984, the
GoBots were built by Bandai for Tonka.
While Tonka had experienced many
success stories in its long history, nothing compared to the incredible sales
generated by these toys. The GoBots
were ordinary-looking toys that were
able to transform into a robot by moving a few of its parts into different positions. The introduction of Tonka's
GoBots had a major impact on how
children played with toys. Here was a
dual-function toy with a whole new
play dimension never before experienced by children of any generation.
A two-month tour featuring the
GoBots kicked off in Boston on July
17, 1984, and covered several major
U.S. cities. The promotion had a 3.5-
foot-tall GoBot deliver emergency
shipments of GoBots to several toy
stores. Stawasz Public Relations of
New York coordinated the tour,
which used the talents of one of
the nation's premier robot author-
ities, Robert Malone. The GoBots
were so successful during the

Go Bots were able to transform from
a vehicle into a robot.
Lloyd L. Laumann collection

Dolls

Royal Princess Sparkle No. 7701

Whisper™
the Secret
Wish Fairy

NEW!

Star Fairies Asst. No. 7700

Royal Princess Sparkle No. 7701
- Beautifully dressed in shimmering
  gown and royal cape
- Polarized wings change color when
  through child-size wand
- Brush, child-size wand, doll-size w
  and posing stand included

Ages: 4 and up   Master Pack: 12

Star Fairies Asst. No. 7700
- Star Fairies make your wishes co
- Beautifully-dressed fantasy fashio
- Fully-articulated with Twist 'n Tu
  and bendable knees

On moonlit nights, when the air is filled with magic and the sky sprinkled with stars, that's the time when Star Fairies are born. They come from falling stars. And take little girls to a world where wishes come true.

Star Fairies™ dolls are manufactured and sold under license from HORNBY HOBBIES, LIMITED.

Spice™
the Energy Fairy

True Love™
the Love Fairy

...tsong™
Dream Fairy

Jazz™
the Talent Fairy

Sparkle™
the Star Fairy Princess

Luxurious rooted hair for brushing and
styling play
Detachable wings snap on and off to change
costumes
Each doll comes with color-coordinated
wings, fanciful costume, brush, wand and
posing stand

Assortment includes:
Sparkle, the Star Fairy Princess, reigns over her
fairy helpers.
Nightsong, the Dream Fairy, is a sweet song in
the night as she makes little girls' sweet dreams
come true.

Jazz, the Talent Fairy, helps little girls express
their creative talents and all that jazz.
Spice, the Energy Fairy, adds a little spice to
little girls' lives as she helps them get things
done.
True Love, the Love Fairy, shows little girls how
to look deep inside others to see their true
goodness.
Whisper, the Secret Wish Fairy, silently goes
about her task of making little girls' secret
wishes come true.

Ages: 4 and up
Master Pack: 24

69

year that many retail stores actually asked Tonka to discontinue advertising for the GoBots because they couldn't keep them on store shelves. Articles praising the wonders of the GoBots were written in every major newspaper in America. Success for the GoBot line even found its way into television, as Tonka hired Hanna-Barbera, one of Hollywood's leading cartoon producers, to create a series of cartoon shows to air during "GoBot Week" around the nation. The series breathed life into the characters of the GoBots, and more episodes were created.

In September 1984, another new product diversified Tonka's offerings even more. The Star Fairies mini doll line was marketed as a fantasy toy for girls. The Star Fairies were led by Sparkle, a special princess who listened to the wishes of little girls and selected one of the other Star Fairies to make the wish come true. Each Star Fairy had its own identity and specialized in different

Star Fairies were a Tonka product that appeared in 1985.
Lloyd L. Laumann collection

NEW!

Pound Puppy Put-Ons™ No. 7806

Pound Puppies (and later, Pound Purries) were very popular in the mid- to late 1980s.

Lloyd L. Laumann collection

areas. They all lived on Sunshine Isle, and the toy was marketed to offer something for the girls along with the GoBots for boys.

For 1985, Tonka introduced another toy that would go on to produce incredible profits during its successful tenure. Pound Puppies were cute and lovable puppies based on a design by Mike Bowling, who had been making them by hand with a double-knit fabric. When Rob Steiner, a former president of Kenner Toys, approached Tonka president Steve Shank with an agreement to market Pound Puppies, the idea was reviewed by Tonka's market research department, which indicated the toy would receive a strong reception in the

In 1987, Tonka introduced the Aurora dolls.
Lloyd L. Laumann collection

AURORA

The Future Looks Beautiful!

The future is here! Introducing Aurora™, Tonka's exciting new line of high-fashion dolls. The Aurora line has the beautiful ultra-modern look and style that will become the rage with little girls across the nation. They're the futuristic 11½" poseable dolls that offer the ultimate in fashion, glamour and beauty.

Each Aurora doll is jointed to move just like the world's top fashion models! Their sleek, shining metallic or glittering crystal bodies and sparkling, jeweled eyes are like nothing else! All have silky, radiantly colored hair that can be combed and styled in the latest fashions. And every Aurora doll comes with a hot, outrageous outfit of shimmering fabric and delicate lace for dressing/undressing.

Aurora dolls are available in four hot styles:
Aurora™, with radiant gold body and blond hair
Mira™, with lusterous silver body and blue hair
Lustra™, with shimmering pewter body and lavender hair
Chrysta™, with sparkling crystal body and pink hair
Accessories for the Aurora line include six stunning outfits that will fit all Aurora dolls.

Aurora™ from Tonka. The future's never looked so good!
Aurora™ doll assortment #6700
Aurora™ clothing assortment #6701

Tonka®

The trademarks Tonka, Aurora and all related character marks are owned by Tonka Corporation. © 1987 Tonka Corporation.

Trucks that stand the test of time!

Mighty Tonka™ Dump-Silver Edition

#2500

- Vacuum metalized Mighty Tonka™ Dump Truck
- Limited Quantity—individually numbered and registered
- Made with steel in the U.S.A.
- Special Silver Anniversary Package

Ages: 3 and up
Master Pack: 4
Package Dimensions: 22¾ x 9¾ x 12⅛

Tonka **Products**
A TONKA DIVISION
Minnetonka Corporate Center
6000 Clearwater Drive
Minnetonka, MN 55343
Toll Free 1-800-347-3628
In Minnesota Call Collect
(612) 936-3300

market. Several refinements were made to the original concept, including replacing the double-knit fabric with velour, and by 1985, Pound Puppies had taken the nation by storm. An appearance of the Pound Puppies on *Good Morning America* in October 1984 drew over 500 phone calls from around the country. The Pound Puppies controlled the stuffed animal market for the next several years and generated huge profits for Tonka.

The mid-1980s found Tonka in sound financial shape with great sales of Pound Puppies, GoBots, Star Fairies, and its dependable line of toy trucks. Licensing for its products also contributed to the bottom line. In 1985, licensing of products for the GoBots alone numbered 43, while the Pound Puppies had 36. There were lunch boxes, balloons, beach towels, sneakers, cards, books, pajamas, and watches that featured Tonka's products.

On April 7, 1986, Tonka announced a 3-for-2 common stock split, which resulted in 6.6 million shares outstanding. With a clear identification of products that consumers would buy, Tonka reported net revenues of an astounding $244.4 million for 1985. For 1986, Tonka launched a major European expansion effort to further its market penetration. Tonka recruited four former Mattel executives that already had high profile ties in the United

1985 Dump Truck.
Dennis David

For the 25th anniversary of the Mighty Dump, Tonka produced a silver edition for the occasion.
Lloyd L. Laumann collection

This semi truck received a special mural for Tonka's 50th anniversary.

Lloyd L. Laumann collection

Kingdom toy industry. Back in the United States, the El Paso facility converted to a new method of manufacturing pioneered by the automotive industry. The "Just in Time" method manufactured products in steps without warehousing parts between the various processes. For instance, a Mighty Dump would have its body stamped, move straight to deburring, and then onto paint without any time spent on the shelf. This lowered inventories of painted metal and plastic parts. The reduction in warehousing and labor costs increased productivity, and this new method saved dollars needed for other investments.

1991 Georgia Power Line Truck
Lloyd L. Laumann collection

Tonka redesigned its Mighty line for 1987 with a renewed emphasis on greater ease of play and contemporary styling. Improvements were made to the cranking systems for raising and lowering the bucket on the Mighty Tonka Crane, and all construction vehicles were marketed under a central theme called Tonka Trax. The new style carried a tough look that spoke directly to the durability standards established many years before by Charles M. Groschen and his design team of the original No. 3900 Mighty Dump Truck.

Tonka continued to expand its holdings. On October 16, 1987, Tonka acquired 95 percent of Kenner Parker Toys, and the sale was completed with the balance of shares tendered on December 8, 1987. While Tonka may have been a global company as early as the 1970s, the size and scope of the Tonka Toy Company was now astounding. Global sales were several hundred million dollars per year, and to a new generation of children around the world, the Tonka name was synonymous with products of all shapes and sizes. While the company still manufactured toy trucks, its vast array of other products also contributed to a large percentage of profits.

Tonka had spent the bulk of the 1980s pursuing acquisitions to become the third-largest toy company, but in May 1991, Tonka was officially acquired by the toy giant Hasbro Inc. Under Hasbro's stewardship, Tonka has continued to prosper and grow. The name is still

Dale Olseth

Dale Olseth was hired by Tonka in 1971 as a replacement for Russ Wenkstern, who was going to retire. He remembers being impressed by Wenkstern and Charles Groschen. "Between the two of them, they knew every single employee's name, and we're talking about hundreds of people," Olseth said. He learned a lot from working with Wenkstern, including that Tonka's greatest asset was its people. "Of all of the businesses that I've led, none had positive morale like that of Tonka," he said.

Olseth was part of the team that is credited with significantly increasing Tonka's business when he instituted a direct-sales marketing strategy for Tonka. "Previous to that, Tonka employed manufacturer representatives," he said. When Olseth started working at Tonka, he questioned why Sears accounted for only 1 percent of Tonka's toy output. "Sears was a retail giant, and they surely had the means to sell more Tonka toys," Olseth said. He flew to Chicago and met with a Sears executive who said that Tonka took too much time to unveil its new line of toys. The Sears executive said, "By the time we see what Tonka has at the February toy show in New York, we've already made our decision on what we're buying for the coming year." According to Olseth, "Sears asked us to back everything up by one year and send salespeople direct from the factory." The results didn't take long, and about one year later, Sears accounted for 12 percent of Tonka's toy output. "Direct marketing of our own products was a good move for us," he said.

Olseth left Tonka in 1976 to become president and CEO of Medtronics, a company specializing in heart pacemakers and other medical products. "I went from toys to heart products, and it certainly was a change," he said. Olseth still lives in the Twin Cities and is still active in business and civic events, and he remembers his years at Tonka with great fondness. "Leaving Tonka was one of the hardest decisions in my life, but I enjoyed my time there and I was proud to be part of the Tonka family."

synonymous with rugged toy trucks and durable construction toys. The look has changed, as well as the ratio of steel to plastic, but the modern look of Tonka's trucks is still impressive. The original concept of quality and durability has been carried over to the present day with Hasbro's introduction of Tonka Tough Truck Adventures. The Heroes with Horsepower toys are equipped with T-Shift technology that unlocks hidden features, which turns these trucks into the ultimate play adventure. These Tonka Tough Trucks also come with a bonus DVD featuring CGI animation. Big wheels and animated features give the newer designs a look that appeals to the child of the twenty-first century. Hasbro has dedicated its resources to maintain the reputation of Tonka, and children everywhere can still grow up with the Tonka brand name.

The Tonka story itself is one of an incredible journey. From the humble confines of a small schoolhouse, to a giant corporation that fills the needs of children everywhere, "Tonka" remains a household word for strength and durability in toys. The vision of Lynn E. Baker, Avery Crounse, and Al Tesch has come full circle.

Opposite: Mound plant, circa 2003.
Dennis David

Fast Fact

THE ORIGINAL FOUNDERS

Although the size of the Tonka Toy Company is truly amazing, there was a time when it was just a vision of the three original founders. The three men worked together for only six years, but in that time, they assembled a team that took Tonka from the little schoolhouse to practically every home in America and beyond.

Avery F. Crounse was the most formally educated of the three, and although he left Tonka in 1952, he can be credited with arranging the financing that got Mound Metalcraft started. After leaving the company at age 72, Crounse focused on geneological research for his family lines. Crounse passed away on June 12, 1960, at the age of 80.

Alvin F. Tesch, the talent behind the actual metal fabrication of Tonka's early products, was a jack-of-all-trades. He left Tonka in 1952 to pursue other interests. He had a 57-year career in the machine trade in the Minneapolis area. According to Venita Cronk, his daughter, Tesch was a quiet man. "He never spoke much about his years with Tonka, and we tried to get him to write his memoirs, but he never got around to it." Tesch passed away on December 5, 2000, at the age of 85.

The only original founder who maintained a presence at Tonka well into its successful years was Lynn E. Baker. As a former salesman of anything from cars to industrial machines, Baker was the driving force to promote the toys of Mound Metalcraft. When Crounse and Tesch left in 1952, Baker assembled the team that led Tonka to the success it enjoyed in the 1960s and beyond. Baker always carried a notebook to jot down notes and ideas about future Tonka designs. He had an incredible eye for knowing what would sell, and he was usually right. In his latter years, Baker split his time between a house in Florida and his lakefront home in Minnesota. He passed away on January 4, 1964.

The three men who started the Tonka Toy Company were very different from one another, but perhaps this difference is what made the company work. Each was very talented, and each had his own opinion about how things should be. Today, as children glide down the aisles of any given toy store and see the exciting designs of Tonka's products, they are completely unaware of the names Crounse, Tesch, and Baker. All over the world on every Christmas morning, big smiles overcome the face of children as they wrap their hands around their first Tonka toy. Surely, the three original founders would be pleased.

Epilogue

1966 No.537 Giant Dozer.
Lee Klancher

THE TONKA STORY TOOK ON A NEW DIMENSION WHEN IT WAS ACQUIRED BY HASBRO IN 1991. THE name still lives on, but the faces and products have changed. Tonka has faired well as part of the Hasbro Inc. family, and the Tonka name still generates millions of dollars in sales every year. The Tonka Toy Company, as it stands today, is part of a global corporation with manufacturing facilities in many countries. The little company started by three men in a school on the shores of Lake Minnetonka after World War II has grown beyond anyone's expectations, and millions of children have been happier for it.

Through the years, Tonka went through a lot of ups and downs, but its quality was never in question, as all of their toys lived up to the company's reputation. Tonka also survived several management shakeups that would have put other companies out of business. Certainly two of the original founders leaving six years after the company started could have been detrimental, and the turbulent management years of the 1970s and 1980s were a trying time. With all of these factors present, we must look to the one constant that never wavered throughout Tonka's years in Mound, Minnesota: the employees.

In 1971, Tonka executives Russ Wenkstern and Dale Olseth communicated to all Tonka employees. In it, they outlined the goals of the company, which was titled the Tonka creed. It read:

"Tonka Corporation will strive to serve the best interests of its stockholders, employees, customers, and communities through the following objectives:

-To perpetuate and stress the profitable growth of the corporation.
-To maximize return on investment and minimize the dilution of equity through effective use of resources consistent with sound business and financial practices.
-To provide for employees an environment conducive to personal development, satisfaction, and financial security.
-To develop and market products which are high quality, safe, and offer sound value to the customer.
-To strive for leadership in the markets served by the corporation.
-To exercise the highest level of commercial honor and personal ethics in all activities.
-To be identified by the public as a strong, fair, and growing company.
-To protect the ecology and to conserve the use of natural resources.
-To be a respected and active member of the business and social community.
-To pursue excellence in all company endeavors including people, product, facilities, and policies."

Russ Wernstern presents 10 shares of Tonka stock to Gwen Cressy during Tonka's employee 25th anniversary celabration on October 27, 1972. Gwen was one of three employess to receive this 25-year anniversary gift.
Lloyd L. Laumann Collection

This company creed was recognized by all as the outline for Tonka's day-to-day business, and there were many signs posted throughout the vast Mound manufacturing facility, and also in the Spring Park warehouse that explained this creed in simpler terms. The signs read:

TONKA IS <u>PROUD</u> OF ITS
...PEOPLE
...PRODUCT
...PLANT

Today we can only look back in wonder at the history of a toy company that truly exemplifies the American dream. The Tonka story is not a story of the company itself, but it is the combination of several thousand stories. In the end, it was not the effort of one man or one machine. It was the combined effort of a group of people who took pride in their work. No problem was too large to solve, and no problem ever occurred that couldn't be overcome by hard work. Housewives blazed a path for all to follow, and farmers born with a talent for fixing things made Tonka what it was during those years in Mound, Minnesota. The real story of Tonka's years in Mound, Minnesota, is found in the hearts of the men and women that worked there.

The city of Mound, Minnesota, looks much the same today as it did on that last day of toy production in 1983. The Tonka facility still stands, but it has been divided into areas that are leased to several different companies.

There are many people who drive up Shoreline Drive in Mound and take note of the expansive plant that was once the home of Tonka Toys, but just a short distance away children play on the shores of the great lake that gave the company its name. While the children play, the memories of the plant are lost to time.

Index